RIDE IT!

The Complete Book of

BIG BIKE RACING

Printed and bound in England by the publishers

Published by
J H HAYNES & CO LTD
SPARKFORD YEOVIL SOMERSET ENGLAND

Soft cover edition **ISBN 0 85696 178 7**
Hard cover edition — *a FOULIS MOTORCYCLING BOOK* — **ISBN 0 85429 220 9**

Editor Jeff Clew
Production/Design Tim Parker
Illustration Terry Davey

RIDE IT!

The Complete Book of
BIG BIKE RACING

Jim Swift

Foulis

Contents

Foreword

As far as I am concerned the 750cc class is the Formula One of motorcycle racing. I have raced in every class and I consider it to be racing at its best.

Although I gained my racing ground work on 125cc machines, and came near to winning a world championship on a Suzuki in this class back in 1971, I would certainly never go back to small bikes. After my first race on a 750, I was well and truly bitten by the big bike bug.

The 750 and 500 classes are the only ones that really interest me now, and even though this means only one ride at a Grand Prix, for example, it does not bother me. I simply have no interest whatsoever in racing 250 or 350 machines. Two rides would be great, of course, and I would love to see the 750s come in to the World Championship stakes.

It will only be a matter of time, in my opinion, before the 750 class gets the full recognition it deserves. It must be best for the manufacturers who go racing, to help with the development of road bikes, and to promote their sales. The power and speed of the big machines must keep everyone on their toes. The tyre manufacturers are always pressing ahead with new designs and compounds for their products which, in time, must mean better tyres for safety and wear for the ordinary motorcyclist.

The chain manufacturers too, must get more benefit from 750cc racing, with the surging horsepower testing their products to the full. In fact, everyone associated with racing machines must get more help with progress from the big bikes.

When it comes to organiser promotion, the 750 class again comes out on top. Although race spectators enjoy close racing, there is definitely an added thrill if that wheel-to-wheel battle comes in the big capacity race. The sheer speed of the bikes, the thought of the riders controlling two-wheel power houses with potential top speeds of 170mph or more, must turn on the excitement more than the smaller capacity machines.

Because of this, sponsorship is attracted more easily to the big bike events. For example, the *Motor Cycle News* Superbike Championship has attracted numerous financial backers over the years, and the series has built up to become one of the most important in the calendar. It is certainly the premier British championship event now and one which manufacturers and riders alike both set out to win. Personally, I want to win the series again this year; missing out on a hat trick of wins in the championship was one of the biggest disappointments for me, last year.

Although the 750 class has still a long way to go, as far as recognition is concerned outside Britain, it already has a magic all of its own, world-wide. You have only to consider events like Daytona and the Imola 200. The fans spend their hard earned cash to travel hundreds of miles to be there, and the factories try everything they know to provide the winning machine. It is the draw of the big bikes. I don't want to be rude, but I can hardly imagine 125 or even 250cc machines attracting that much attention.

Despite calls from some quarters to cut down the race speeds in the interest of safety, I am still confident that the future of our sport is in the 750 class. It is impossible to stop development and advancement. My worst crash, the much publicised 180mph Daytona prang, was on a 750, but it has not turned me against them, or their power.

If the FIM, as the governing body of motorcycle racing, puts a hurdle in the way like limiting carburettor sizes or anything else aimed at cutting power, then it will simply add to the challenge of improving efficiency in some other area. 750 racing is the tops for riders, spectators and organisers.

The thrill of a machine capable of 185mph has to be experienced to be enjoyed. Like a super girl, there is nothing quite like it!

BARRY SHEENE

Preface

It is a matter of personal opinion as to what constitutes a big bike. In fact the title of this book, being decided before I was invited to write it even, has dictated a few problems which I am not entirely certain I can solve whilst, at the same time, keeping to the basic scheme of things.

Our entire theme is that of road racing, and since a big bike, to me, is something over 600cc — a relatively useful capacity from which to draw the line — I shall endeavour to ignore all smaller models. That I fail in this intent will be obvious to all as they progress through the chapters; but I make no apology since the term big bike has been relative to all stages of history in a variety of contexts.

Although the concept of a big bike is as old as the motorcycle itself, the modern terminology Superbike and Powerbike usefully describes the type of machine we have in mind. Funnily enough, there will be some readers who will recall the original Powerbike as being a Francis Barnett motorised cycle, and even in more latter years Suzuki had a 36cc machine with a similar connotation, both of which are far removed from today's idiom. But the modern terms, created to provide an image which the industry lacked, personify an era of motorcycle sport which future historians will look back upon as fondly as present ones do to the halcyon days of the fifties. The present-day 750s all owe their development to the sport; the Japanese industrial titans are a product of the way the motorcycle has developed with the advance of time, even though they were not generally part of it themselves.

I find it undesirable, therefore, to ignore the chronology necessary to indicate the various stages of the sport. True, there is little big bike identity before the last few years, with the emphasis invariably on the 500cc machine, but the modern big bike is a product of the way racing has forced its development through various stages. A prime example is the Isle of Man events which have survived as an unbroken record, war years excepted, of British racing; whose records themselves are essentially those of British sport as a whole. Without this background the reader loses much, the *nolens volens* attitudes and problems which beset many an honest organiser are even mirrored today when we should know better.

It is a problem, nevertheless, to know how rigidly to treat the subject of history, whose significance can be as elusive as an Ali Shuffle.

To extract readable essentials with maximum interest is not as easy as it sounds, particularly as we have in mind a period spanning some seventy years; seventy of the most interesting and formative years of development. The period was interrupted by two world wars, and the resultant economic and political unrest both at home and abroad had a major effect on the world's markets. Not only do we need to understand our own development but those of other countries, particularly the United States, whose destiny was to combine with our own to produce some of the world's greatest races.

It is a moot, and very arguable point as to who has done most for whom within the sport; whether road racing could have existed without the late influence of the Japanese, or whether our own industry would have reacted to the vacuum and produced the type of machine which is in such demand the world over, whether road or racing. Certainly the American market has been responsible for the huge interest shown at present by the Japanese who have backed their judgement with a competitive interest second to none. At the conclusion of the roaring fifties the Japanese manufacturers pulled out of road racing *en bloc.* They could still do it again, but the highly receptive markets for the big bike will not allow them to do so quite as lightly as before. If nothing else, the Japanese have proved beyond doubt that, as the world's markets needed the 50cc — 250cc machines for commuter transport some years ago, they need the big 750cc today. That they have captured a large chunk of the world's markets in such a short space of time is not really surprising when you appreciate how slow we are, in Europe, in assessing future demand.

JIM SWIFT
Mallory Park
Leicester

Acknowledgements

In compiling this book I have to thank a number of people whose contributions have been equally important in providing what I hope will be an enjoyable addition to the bookshelves of two-wheeled enthusiasts the world over. Mike Turner has produced the majority of photographs of the British scene and his work adorns most of the pages in this book. John Player Photographic Library allowed me to poach from their reserves and Andrew Marriott added some of his own collection for which I suspect Player's, and Peter Taylor, should gain credit! Mike Nicks delved into his files and came up with useful shots of the American scene, particularly Daytona, Ontario and Ascot, while Chris Carter, in his own inimitable way, produced the now famous recorder, when both Cecotto and Cooper were around. Much of the credit must go to Jackie White for the chapter on Suzuki. I couldn't have written it without her notes which put truth into an otherwise issue of conjecture. Reg Lee and Jim Ward came to my aid when I needed it most and various other photographs have been provided from the libraries of manufacturer and individual alike, particularly Norrie Whyte for his endurance photographs and Mick Woollett.

Lastly, I am undecided as to whether or not to thank my father! If he had bought the Square Four instead of the Vincent I doubt that I would have been in a position to write what has turned out to be a rather lengthy epistle. Not that it will all be published; but the effort over twelve months has made me realise that to write the 'complete book' is a task which demands far more time than I have given it, and far more room at home, where a vigilant wife not only removed the cobwebs and dust, but also managed to make me feel less than ideal at times when duty called me back to putting words on paper! I must thank her patience for allowing me to use not one room, but every room in the house, all at the same time!

1 Early impressions

Like most readers I, too, have suffered the joys of motorcycling to a greater or lesser extent, although I cannot pretend to lifelong experience. Unlike my father, I didn't start life in a raincoat and beret on one of our now lost heritages, although I did manage to own one or two. Number one never got off the workbench and number two eventually persuaded me that there were great advantages in having four wheels!

Memory is blurred of course and, at times, strictly out of sequence. When you have to sit down to think about what the highlights were in your life, it's funny how misty and unimportant they seem. My father had joined the Military Police as a TA before the war in order to avoid foot-slogging the muddy paths of Europe. The motor cycle press were full of the advantages at the time, with both Malcolm Campbell and De Montford-Sebag openly inviting people to join the Territorial Army. It was obvious that war was going to break sooner or later so he decided that he would prefer to have a motorcycle under him. Hostilities concluded, he put in an order for an Ariel Square Four, which was delayed far too long for his liking, and I can vaguely remember the north London firm of Humphrey's selling him a Vincent Rapide instead. Probably that one factor had more influence on my life than anything else because there is a very true saying within the motorcycling movement that "once a Vincent owner always a Vincent owner". I was dragged along to Vincent Owners' Club meetings and eventually ended up on the organising side of motorcycle racing through the contacts made. I still manage to spot original members amongst the spectators and officials today. They may have arrived by car but the front still sports the easily recognisable VOC badge.

It was inevitable that I was destined to follow in my father's footsteps. I remember that he bought me a model J HRD to keep me off the streets. It was a complete non-runner and was towed by my father's combination, drunkenly wallowing with my uncle on board, from St. Pancras Station, where it had been sent, to the basement of a Stoke Newington undertakers that my father owned at the time! How the journey was made I don't honestly know. It was late evening and the towed vehicle had no lights. It was almost a wreck, but it had an intrinsic value which may be more understandable to me today than it was at the time. I spent my school holidays earning enough money to get it on the road, a cause which was about as lost as a grain of sand in a gale. It did teach me what the innards looked like but since I have never had to work on a JAP engine since, it proved a waste of time! Perhaps it served its purpose, though what happened to it I cannot remember. I do remember vividly the occasion my father and I went up to Sheffield to pick up a spare engine, and of the chap we were buying it from cutting through some very excellent Reynolds 541 tubing with a hacksaw held in his bare hands. Smoke poured off the blade, which curled up when he let it go!

After the machine that never was came a 500 Series A HRD on which I took my motorcycle test. I can remember to this day going along to see my old headmaster to ask for time off. He asked me many questions about my hobbies and what I wanted to do when I left school — I think I wanted to join the police at the time — and eventually was sufficiently satisfied to let me off for the afternoon. I am conceited enough to boast that I passed first time and was sufficiently smug to tell him so next time we met. It was a 1935 model with the recognisable external hairpin valve-gear which was typical of the model, and even in the fifties it was good enough to give fair account of itself against much later machines. Later, I bought my uncle's 600 Royal Enfield Meteor, the predecessor of the Super Meteor, Constellation and Interceptor, which was my first real taste of a smooth twin. It had an unhappy knack of releasing the steel plug inserts in the alloy cylinder-heads every time I took the plugs out, which occasioned taking the heads off to get them back. Platinum spark plugs were used to obviate

A remarkable piece of 'big bike' engineering was my 1936 HRD Rapide. It was capable of speeds in excess of 100mph when I owned it in the late 1960s. On one rare occasion it was put to the test — the GPO had to rescue me, sealing a split in the fuel tank

the problem, which were not changed for about 5,000 miles, while the carbon built up around them! I think it was eventually sold with these still in. It had other characteristics of a bovine ancestry and the problem that, to change a tyre on the back wheel, you literally had to block up the stand to lift it sufficiently far off the ground to work. It was a rather wet night that I had a puncture in a racing cover and that was that — it just had to go. Some time later I bought another Series A HRD, the 1000cc plumbers nightmare, so named because of all its external oilpipes. It kept my boots waterproof and itself rust-free, and many happy hours were spent ruminating over its many complexities, some of which I never did understand.

I am, and always have been, a big bike fanatic. I get no real enjoyment out of owning small capacity machines, regardless of their fine qualities. I have owned and ridden many different varieties and models, but the one that stands out the most is probably the late Mick Bennett's racing Vincent which I sneaked around Silverstone for lap after lap, until my conscience caught up with me and I retired abashed back to the paddock. I took Dave Degens Barcelona 650 Dresda on the New York to London air race, which proved a marvellous experience, particularly after having been let down by a privately owned 750 Dunstall in the middle of the night, miles from anywhere. A slight twist of the throttle on any big machine and it will accelerate away without any need to rev its innards out or to change down into a lower gear.

I am the first to admit that times have changed. Even the small 250s have that extra quality today that they didn't have ten years ago. There is no way that you can compare the Ariel Arrow with the modern Yamaha counterpart. Although the Arrow was raced in long distance races and the odd one or two people tried to join two twins together in an attempt to be futuristic, there is no possible comparison with the development programme of Yamaha. But the big Vincent, to me, is the very epitomy of motorcycling. A machine which ceased manufacture in 1965 is still powering solos and sidecars on the racing circuits of the world. True, they are declining in number, but I wonder how many of the present big bikes will be around even ten years from now.

2 From drawing board to race track

Motorcycling has long been the cheapest form of motorised transport and will continue to be so in the foreseeable future, while engineers can continue to produce such a highly efficient internal combustion engine and marry it successfully into a frame. The modern motorcycle is tractable, giving supreme mobility under varied conditions and requirements, with a performance unheard of even ten years ago. And yet the whole concept of a motorcycle has occurred as much by accident as design and it would be difficult to imagine a more arduous exercise if one had to start from scratch, putting an engine into a frame with a wheel at each end. Frame design has barely kept up with development of the engine. It was not so many years ago that Mike Hailwood had tremendous difficulty with the frame of his 500 Honda. The standard racing frame was very little more than a moped design, a half loop into which was bolted that massive engine. It handled like a camel, wallowing from side to side even on the straight. Under braking, it twisted and bent in the middle as though hinged, and more than once in every race threatened to dump Mike in the dirt. It seemed as though strengthening struts used to appear every time it was brought out, but to no avail. The basic structure was unsound and no amount of playing around with spare metal and a welding torch could remedy the inadequacy. The engine was too powerful for the frame and that was all there was to it. Perhaps it had been wrongly mounted, but the astonishing fact was that Honda didn't make another frame, in spite of the fact that Mike annoyed them with his constant efforts to get a better frame made privately.

It is a matter of history that whenever a machine has been manufactured it has invariably been put into competition of one form or another. People are like that the world over, the quest for competition being stronger than life itself. This, therefore, takes the subject of big bike racing back to early this century. Capacity of engine did not at first separate one machine from another, but it was quickly realised that horse power unfairly utilised gave one rider a greater advantage over the other, particularly in view of the fact that the handling characteristics were very much the same for all machines — absolutely terrible.

Motorcycles were just what the name implied, motorised cycles, in the late nineteenth century, being very much a test bed for the development of the internal combustion engine which Dr. Nikolaus Otto patented in 1876. There was a social stigma attached to the early pioneers, who did little to enlighten public opinion. Silencing was open to abuse, not that the term really existed in any case, and the antics of the suddenly uncontained power gave rise to concern. It was no wonder then, that motorcycling got off to the wrong sort of start. Petrol was not easily obtained, so use was restricted to short journeys and racing limited. Frames were rigid and so were the forks, which meant frequent breakages of both. Brakes were little more than cycle calipers, and the tyres, though pneumatic, lacked adhesion — often with fatal consequences. It is worthy of note that John Boyd Dunlop had developed his pneumatic tyre as early as 1888 and his company, today, still keeps pace with the modern development of the motorcycle. The drive to the back wheel of these early machines was hit and miss; driven mainly by a leather belt which slipped badly in wet conditions and, on occasions, broke completely. The roller chain as we know it today wasn't developed until 1894 by Hans Renolds.

It is almost impossible to define where the first organised race took place but most historians agree that the scene was Europe, probably France. Cycling was a popular mode of transport, a rewarding pastime and a popular spectator sport in Europe at the time, and it is certainly true that the closed cycle tracks were used both at home and abroad for the first of the motorised sports. Britain suffered from speed restrictions so, if you wanted to race on the public road, you had either to go abroad or risk heavy fines or even imprisonment if you tried it here. The earliest speed restriction was 4mph, which was quite absurd.

Even today the machines of the distant past have an unusual attraction to rider and spectator alike. This Zenith shows a great deal of renovation work

1907 saw the opening of Brooklands at Weybridge in Surrey, the first of Britain's racing circuits, which provided an opportunity for the British manufacturer to test his machines to their full capabilities. He, at long last, could match his European counterpart by being able to run his machines as fast as he wanted to, for as long as he wanted. Races were organised by the Brooklands Automobile Racing Club between 1907 and 1914, who allowed motorcycles to encroach upon their otherwise car racing programme. A lap of the Brooklands bowl was 2.76688 miles on the fifty foot line (an accuracy much lacking today) which effectively provided a rigorous testing ground for every type of machine, its concrete surface allowing no one to go to sleep. After the first Bemsee meeting the profit was a mere 60p. During the same year the Tourist Trophy started in the Isle of Man, this particular siting being chosen because, although the mainland restriction had been raised from 4mph to 12mph and then to 20mph, the Manx Government had no restrictions. Unlike the mainland they could also close their roads to the public for racing if they chose. Cars had been racing in the Island from 1905, so factors were not unnaturally totally in favour of the link which has continued unabated ever since.

The Marquis de Mouzilly St. Mars, a prominent French pioneer motorcyclist, came forward with a trophy, and the Tourist Trophy was born, so named because it was intended for touring machines and not for the racers which we know today. There was no engine capacity limitation in 1907, neither was there a weight limit. Machines had to be efficiently silenced — 15 years later Brooklands suffered from the same restriction — and standard units fitted, saddle, mudguards and two inch diameter tyres as opposed to the 2.3/8'' to 3'' sizes of the bigger machines. Petrol was restricted, so a degree of compromise on the throttle was necessary. The course used was not the same as that for the cars since it was abundantly apparent that the belt driven machines were not capable of climbing the mountain.

Imagine riding this Bat on the roads or even racing it, without hydraulic suspension

The first world war stopped racing for five years and during this period the motorcycle changed in stature. The common need for speedy dispatch and manoeuvre appealed to both friend and foe alike, and at the end of hostilities a much improved machine emerged, even though the majority of the British factories had been turned over to munitions. Reliability was suddenly recognised as being as important as speed. The war finished in the November of 1918 but a general slump was to make progress a slow struggle for years to come.

The development of the engine had taken a sporting turn. Side-valve engines were about to be supplanted by the overhead valve type and the vee twin was beginning to influence racing in its improved guise. Indian and Harley-Davidson had manufactured production 1000cc models which were recognised as racing machines. America, too, introduced the four cylinder engine which put in a brief appearance, the capacity of the Henderson being 1170cc. In Britain, production engines like the JAP were being used to power all sorts of private enterprises, being used in George Brough's now famous Brough Superior which took Brooklands by storm in the hands of Bert LeVack. Matchless and BSA, amongst others, produced big capacity machines but, in general, the parting of the ways had begun, with more and more emphasis on machines for racing than touring. True, machines were off the production line and within the capabilities of the engineer to be highly tuned, but the drift was towards the complete racer. Although Norton's TT win of 1924 was claimed as a standard machine win it was, perhaps, the last time that such a claim could reasonably be made. It was inevitable, of course, as much then as now. Machines had to develop and there was no way that the limited rule book could help this along, except by avoiding the stagnating complicities which have long been the bain of the racing scene. The Amateur TT was to follow but even this was to fail, not so much because of the machines, but because there was no hope of defining the word amateur.

3 The influence of the Isle of Man races

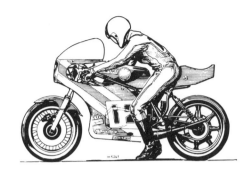

The first TT was run in the Isle of Man in 1907, as a relief from the oppressive mainland restrictions. The International Cup Races, which were run in France from 1904—6, were disappointing from an English point of view and it was decided that every effort should be made to provide an English equivalent. Inferior organisation and a total lack of sportsmanship had almost ruined the 1904 event, the meeting being declared void. It improved in later years but was eventually abandoned. Thus the TT was born, a conception which no one at the time could have imagined would turn into the world's greatest road race.

The fuel limitations imposed for the first race were relaxed in 1908 so that single cylinder machines had enough fuel to average 100mpg and twin cylinder machines 80mpg. Previously it had been far less. Two shaft drive four cylinder machines entered — Belgian F Ns — but these were classed with the twins for the purpose of the fuel allowance. The track was dirt and it was reported that at one point the dust was liberally sprinkled with acid! Petrol restrictions were dropped for 1909, when it was decided to limit the engine size. Twins were allowed to run up to 750cc because they were considered less efficient than the singles; the singles were limited to a maximum of 500cc, a capacity that was to remain as indelible as the bureaucratic thinking behind it. I am firm in the belief that a less restrictive attitude would have advanced development of the motor cycle much quicker. Speeds shot up as riders were relieved of the worry of running out of fuel. Machines suddenly became too fast for the organisers and the Mountain Circuit was introduced, not exactly as we know it today, but a fair resemblance. The surface was so bad that if a rider could stand at the end of a race he was considered to be quite an athlete.

Capacity classes were again altered in 1911. Twins were allowed a capacity of 340cc and singles 300cc, in the new Junior class, whilst in the Senior the twins were reduced to 585cc. Silencers could be dispensed with, except during practice. But manufacturers were showing a little more interest, with entries from AJS, Royal Enfield, Triumph and Matchless. In 1912, the ACU decided that the singles were too handicapped, and allowed the races to be governed by separate capacities. The Senior race limit was to remain at 500cc and the Junior at 350cc. The bigger capacity limit had gone and it was not until 1947 that it returned to the Island in a new guise; new, that is, for 1947, but in point of fact it almost came back where it left off, with standard production machines.

1913 saw the first two-day event. When racing was resumed after the first world war the first massed start was introduced, but it was dropped like a hot brick thereafter.

Riders and manufacturers were said to be against it, but it really wasn't given much of a chance to succeed. Since it was employed in the Ultra Lightweight class — 175cc — it wasn't given fair representation. Massed starts were not used again for twenty-four years. The 175 class was run for two years only and then dropped altogether, because the powers-that-were at the time decided that machines were being developed on the wrong lines; a further indication of how the rule book was used to alter the development of the motorcycle.

The second world war intervened at a most inopportune moment for the works teams and riders. At the termination of hostilities on September 2nd 1945 there was no question of staging another race meeting very early. The fact that it got going once again two years later was entirely due to the Ministry of Fuel and the Petroleum Board, who released fuel supplies for the racing development of the motorcycle, recognising the important part that such development played within the advancing motorcycle industry. A Clubman's category was introduced into the 1947 races providing three separate classes, which included the biggest capacity class yet — for up to 1000cc machines. Only two machines over 500cc entered, one of these being a 600cc Scott.

Massive machinery is not something which was unknown a decade or more ago. Few photographs survive of George Brown in action other than him sprinting 'Super Nero', his blown 1000cc Vincent which he blasts off, in this picture, at Blackbushe in 1964. His Island mount was 'Gunga Din'. George took the sprinter around Silverstone many years ago with very fast 'straights' though slow 'corners'

But the year of 1948 is perhaps our starting point with the subject of big bike racing. Suddenly, we reverted to the stage we were gradually to reach from 1929, with machines entered being basic production machines which the man in the street could go out and buy. I am inclined to the belief that the inclusion of the Clubman's race was for a different reason, however. War had dissipated the number of riders who could take part in what had become a dangerous and almost professional sport. New blood was needed and the riders were carefully selected as being of capable potential with just the right amount of experience. They should not have gained a replica in an International TT or have been placed within the first three places of the Manx Grand Prix, the Isle of Man's 'amateur' road races run entirely by the Manx Motorcycle Club. Any riders claiming such distinction were automatically barred from entering. The rules allowed that the Senior class was for machines over 350cc and up to 1000cc, rather unfairly of course, since it followed obviously that the big machines would be too competitive. Not surprisingly, eleven 1000cc machines faced the starter on June 9th, ten of them Vincents and the remaining one an Ariel Square Four. The odds were stacked pretty highly in favour of the Stevenage twins. Practice times were totally eclipsed in the race, even from a standing kick start which smacked very much of gamesmanship, George Brown knocking a minute and a half off his fastest practice lap. He eventually ran out of petrol and after a long push, finished sixth.

Vincent HRDs took 1st, 2nd, 5th, 6th, 8th, 9th, 11th, 13th, 19th and 26th places, the only 500 Vincent in the race finishing in the creditable eleventh position. Reliability, and their remarkable handling for such a heavy machine, coupled with the sheer power of the engine, had won them their first major laurels. It was also significant for the sport as a whole because, although the Clubman's races eventually suffered the same fate as all the other so-called 'production' machine races, it did put manufacturers back in the public eye where the public could express and identify with machines on the track.

It was evident after the 1948 races that the rules would have to be changed, giving the 1000cc machines a class of their own. In the event, the segregation of the big bikes was all rather pointless, as the speeds of the 500s compared very favourably and would have given a 500 a win overall. The reason for this was obvious. Unlike the 1948 races, which were run over four laps, with a compulsory pit refuelling stop after two laps, the 1949 races were reduced to three laps, and refuelling prohibited. This meant that the big bikes couldn't open up as much as they had before if they wished to conserve enough fuel to finish the race. Fuel tanks had to be perfectly standard so there was no question of being able to carry more fuel to counteract the restriction. It was all a bit of a farce and at least one rider ran out of gas.

The distance for 1950 was put back to four laps and machine modifications permitted. Eleven machines started in a race run under poor visibility, which resulted in several accidents. The 1000 class was dropped in 1951 due to the poor number of entries, a state which affected the meeting as a whole.

The Clubman's TT races, which had commenced in 1947 for classes catering for 250cc, 350cc and 500cc machines, allayed fears that novice riders were being put at risk over the intricate Mountain Circuit. Why the amateur races hadn't succeeded in doing this I don't really know. The 250cc category was dropped due to a lack of interest as, of course, was the 1000cc class. Before long, the organisers were finding it increasingly difficult to preserve the essential nature of the races, which still hoped to provide production racing at a price all could afford. At the end of 1954 things stood in the balance. The total race schedule, which included practice as well as racing, was already overlong, with spectator interest decidedly on the wane. Domination of the 500cc Class by the senior Gold Star BSA was a mirror of earlier Vincent victories, but the BSA had become a production racer with its clip-on bars, sharp cam profiles and most other 'extras' which had already spelt doom to the Amateur TT. The regulations were tightened and, to preserve valuable time, the Clubman's Trophy, as it became known, was transferred to the 10.79 mile Clypse Course where it joined the Ultra-lightweight and Lightweight TTs.

In 1956, a last ditch attempt was made by the ACU to preserve the Clubman's Trophy by changing back to the Mountain Circuit. Although there was an improvement in the number of entries there was little evidence of interest from manufacturers. In 1955 only twenty three entries had been received for the senior class and spectator interest reached an even lower ebb. 1956 saw the last of the Clubman's races in the Isle of Man and, although it was resurrected in the 1960s at Silverstone for one year only, it was run during a printing strike which effectively ruined any chances of a respectable gate. After a heavy financial loss it was dropped like a hot potato. Later still, it was run at Oulton Park but never proved successful. Rather like the Manx GP it was found impossible to keep to the original theme of running a popular event for basic production machines.

Clubman's Tourist Trophy Results

1948   350—1000cc

1st	J. D. Daniels	(Vincent HRD)	1hr 52m 29.6s	80.51mph
2nd	F. P. Heath	(Vincent HRD)	1hr 53m 49.0s	79.58mph
3rd	C. A. Stevens	(Norton)	1hr 59m 3.4s	76.07mph
Record Lap:	G. Brown (Vincent HRD) in 27m 24s at 82.65mph			

1949   1000cc

1st	D. G. Lashmar	(Vincent HRD)	1hr 29m 1.8s	76.30mph
2nd	J. Wright	(Vincent HRD)	1hr 33m 27.6s	72.68mph
3rd	P. C. Wilson	(Vincent HRD)	1hr 34m 6.6s	72.19mph
Record Lap:	C. Horn in 26m 28.0s at 85.57mph			

1950   1000cc

1st	A. Phillips	(Vincent HRD)	1hr 55m 18.0s	78.58mph
2nd	S. Alexander	(Vincent HRD)	2hrs 00m 52.2s	74.94mph
3rd	F. J. Young	(Vincent HRD)	2hrs 05m 39.4s	72.08mph
Record Lap:	A. Phillip in 27m 57s at 81.00mph			

Team members for a time — John Cooper and Peter Williams

4 Production racing– the birth of the Manx Grand Prix, Production and Formula 750 races

Production machine racing is a miscellany of ideas aimed towards two targets. On the one hand it should encourage both private owners and manufacturers to take a competitive interest in racing, and, on the other, it should encourage the development of the normal road-going motorcycle to the eventual benefit of the average member of the public. That it does both is obvious, but, as in most cases, there are various shades of grey.

Motorcycle racing, as a whole, cannot exist without an infiltration of young blood. The ability to race a street machine has given a vast number of people a cheap and enjoyable introduction into the racing game at reasonable expense; the rules and regulations have been devised to this end. Throughout the history of racing people have raced all sorts of street machines, modified to take into account safety factors and regulations, and, for the most part, they have competed amicably alongside the more forceful thoroughbred racers. One has only to remember the 1961 Senior TT to recognise the success of some of them; Tom Phillis took the basically standard Norton 88 round the Island at over 100mph. Since the middle and late fifties, however, there has been an attempt to encourage the manufacturer to take an active interest in improving the breed, so to speak, and whereas up to then the street machine was expected to compete side by side with the increasingly quick racers like the Norton Manx and G45 and G50 Matchlesses, some effort was made by the organisers to release them from a burden which was becoming too heavy to carry. In 1959 an attempt was made by the ACU to introduce a Formula One race into the TT programme, barring factory machines. It was run on Saturday May 30th, over three laps of the Mountain Circuit. As a race it was a good one, but it proved little benefit to the idea which, I hasten to add, was a little pointless and historically unsound. The 500cc class was won by Bob McIntyre with Bob Brown second and Terry Shepherd third. The 350cc category was won by Bob's fellow Glaswegian and Joe Pott's stable runner, Alastair King. Bob Anderson came second and the youthful Mike Hailwood third. True, there were none of the Japanese works teams in the race, which probably better equated the competition, but the whole idea seemed to be a bit stick-in-the-mud. While races of this kind were run it almost suggested to the manufacturer that he could sit back and not have the need to develop and catch the emergent motorcycle nations of the world. It was probably at this stage, rather than at any other, that the British manufacturer lost his grip on world markets and requirements.

Racing for street machines, as a class and race in itself, has formed an intermittent part of Club racing over the years. Some Clubs had openly encouraged people to come into the sport, utilising their ride to work machines. Others found no useful purpose in providing races for relatively few people, but it should be recognised that the over-the-counter racers, particularly the 'boy's-racer' 350cc 7R AJS, offered people a pure racing machine out of the showrooms, from as early as 1937, at a price of £87. They were preceded by other models known as the R7, R10 etc. These production racers confused earlier attempts to create a production class as we know it today and there was little need for such a class, since the cost of a pure racer was well within most aspirants' reach.

Within more recent times the racing classes for street machines have provided people with a relatively cheap introduction to racing. Few people who know little of their ability, and even less the bounds of their own enthusiasm, can afford to dive straight into unknown waters. The fact that they can race a basic road machine with very little enforced modification except on the grounds of safety, must invite a degree of competitiveness not apparent at higher levels. Although it is acknowledged that the ability to improve the performance is a basic necessity, many people have found their feet racing such bog-standard machines, often to great effect. Success at the nursery level of Club racing provides incentive to try the slightly faster and more glamorous side of life if and when finances permit, a situation which augers well for the development of the sport. Perhaps I have over-simplified the situation somewhat, but, in general, production racing over the last ten years at least has provided infancy and adolescence, and senile decay too in many cases!

Senility has always existed, which is probably why rules and regulations have been altered, amended and scrapped from time to time. It all boils down to what the aim should be; whether to provide a cheap form of racing in which everyone can be equally mounted — in my opinion an unworkable objective — or whether one should introduce the great potential of spectator appeal which necessarily brings with it the skirmishes which have been apparent over the last few years. How can one keep this form of racing within competitors' pockets and yet, at the same moment, provide a basis for development? No way, is the simple answer. But what can be achieved is a split level; Club racing made possible by a careful restriction on what can and cannot be done to the machine and an International level which sees a basic street machine engine developed as far as it will go. Idealism is fine when you are treating the competitors to a useful and cheap way to go racing but, at spectator level, one has to produce a spectacle which must be improved upon from year to year, if the sport is to go forward. This presents almost insurmountable obstacles.

Most developing manufacturing countries have had a great deal of influence in the production or street motorcycle, to use an American idiom; sensibly, of course, since economic development has been largely linked to success on the racing circuits. To achieve success is not an insular objective; without it the potential market suffers and there comes a point at which it is pointless taking part. If one considers that Suzuki, for instance, started life as a loom manufacturing company in the textile industry in 1909, and it wasn't until 1952 that they produced their first motorcycle, the emergence of Japan comes as quite a surprise. Honda remains the one instance of a company that was first registered as a motorcycle manufacturer as late as 1948, but it wasn't until 1958, ten years later, that their products were exported to Europe. One year later they entered their machines in the Ultra-Lightweight TT and walked off with the manufacturer's prize. Kawasaki exported machines in bulk to America in 1973, to a market that took 82% of its motorcycles from abroad. The Japanese have certainly provided the world with what they needed at the time it was required, a commercial interest which has blossomed and provided the world with that second spectator level of sport which has providently provided increasing benefits for the consumer market. Production racing today is not different in any way from that which has gone before — we just live in a different age where development has virtually outpaced the old-fashioned rules under which it was run.

The problems within the production racing scene have been symptomatic of the various stages of development. Standards have changed as machines have become faster and more reliable. In earlier days, the machines taking part had to race on a prescribed amount of fuel, thus ensuring that the machines remained standard as far as the engine department was concerned. It had dire effects on both the Amateur TT and, later, the Clubman's TT. When the Tourist Trophy races were fifteen years old there was a move to separate the professional and amateur rider. Both terms are relative and there was no real way that the object could suceed. Hindsight is a marvellous facility! It was justly considered that the age of private tuning was being outpaced by the works entered machines, whose standard pace was far superior to any other. Machines being used were mostly factory specials with very professional riders on board, which gave the private runner very little opportunity for competing on anything like equal terms. Secret, exclusive, cam design could no longer be relied upon for additional speed and the consequent development was putting the private owner at a severe disadvantage. On 20th September 1923, the first of the Amateur races were run in the Isle of Man, officially entitled the Amateur Motorcycle Championship Race. Although we are not really concerned with the definition of the word 'amateur' as far as the purpose of this book is concerned, we cannot, in all fairness, leave the progression of the races without comment, since it reflects the situation which has ever been the bain of racing the world over: How to stop racing getting too expensive by the manufacture of machines which few can afford and which few have the opportunity to ride.

An amateur was described thus:

    i) A person who is not at the time of making an entry, or has not been since the first day of January 1923, engaged in the manufacture for sale, or sale or repair, or the exhibition of motor cars or motorcycles, their parts or accessories.

ii) ... has not, since the first day of January 1921, accepted, and undertakes not to accept, any monetary benefit or consideration, or the equivalent thereof, from any person or firm engaged or directly interested in the manufacture for sale of motor cars or motorcycles, their parts or accessories.

iii) ... undertakes not to permit his name to be used in any advertisement of motorcycles, their parts or accessories.

As far as the machine was concerned, effort was made to ensure that it was a stock machine without the expensive alterations being currently embarked upon by leading manufacturers, particularly in the TT which the new Amateur version intended to circumnavigate. Every machine had to be wholly the property of the entrant, whether Club or individual, and have been in his possession on, or before, the first day of July 1923. It also had to be (or have been) of standard origin as listed by the manufacturer, and a catalogue furnished by the entrant at the time the entry was made. Times haven't changed that much as homologation exists today, particularly with regard to the eligibility clause which insisted that the machine should be raced as standard in all respects. The catalogue would provide the guideline, which should allow for only set optional extras. Providing these could be purchased over-the-counter, then they could be fitted.

The first race under these rules was run on September 20th 1923 and covered five laps of the Mountain Circuit, a distance of 188.65 miles. There was only one class, up to 500cc with a separate award going to the leading 350cc rider. The Mayor of Douglas, Councillor A. B. Crookall presented the trophy to the winner, thirty-two year old Len Randles who rode a 1922 long stroke, side-valve, Sunbeam; a machine which he also rode in hill climbs. It was completely standard except for oversize petrol and oil tanks. A single port overhead valve Sunbeam took Len to victory the second year, the event showing a disappointing drop in the number of entries. The date was moved to September 11th in 1925 in an attempt to avoid the poor weather conditions experienced the year before, and no less than forty-eight riders started the race, which was won by a twenty year old naval sub-lieutenant, H.G. Dobbs, riding a 490 Norton. In 1926 the lap distance went up to six laps and was won by Rex Adams, who completed half the race with only one footrest, after having crashed at Kirkmichael. Tim Hunt took the 1927 event on his Norton at only nineteen years of age. In 1928 350cc and 500cc classes were split into two races, rather like the TT which was running in its normal June place. Tim Hunt won the Senior race and another nineteen-year old, W.H.T. Meageen, won the Junior on his own soil. In 1929, the last of the Amateur races, Glaswegian Joe Potts won the Senior race on a Grindlay Peerless, while the Junior went to Eric Lea, following a steward's enquiry which excluded Meageen for reputedly receiving a push.

The Amateur races had come to an end. It was a well known fact that certain riders were in receipt of trade bonuses and encouragement from factories openly thwarted the organiser's attempts to keep the races strictly amateur. It was therefore decided to give up all ideas of keeping to the 'amateur' principles, and the Manx Grand Prix was born the following year to replace the event, at the same time of year but in a different guise. Rider eligibility was simply that riders had to be British or come from Eire. They could not have been entered in any International competition or have held any world speed record since 1920 and the machines used had to be standard models listed by the manufacturer prior to the end of January 1930. The Manx Grand Prix of today is run on exactly the same basis. The term standard, however, came to mean the super developed production racer as did the TT before it and the Clubman's TT after. The street machine disappeared from view very quickly.

On May 6th 1939 a race for production machines was included in *Motor Cycling's* Donington Park meeting on the Leicestershire/Derby borders, much at the insistence of its Editor, Graham Walker, who, more than most, appreciated the problems which faced the beginners to road racing. Even at this stage of our impressive history, the need for this type of racing was still being denied to many people, mainly because the numbers wanting to take advantage were in the minority. It was still not considered important enough to make any real effort to put races on. Many find an identical situation today so there is no way that one can find fault with those decision makers of the past.

Over six thousand spectators came to watch this 1939 event, which was run in almost ideal weather conditions. It was opened by a grand parade of manufacturers riding their own machines, and included such celebrities as Sir Malcolm Campbell and his son Donald, who had ridden their own machines from London to take part in the parade. The race programme included two production machine races, one of which had to be divided into two heats as no less than sixty five entries had been received. There was also a race for pre-1931 machines, to give the older models a chance, a race which was won by a young lad by the name of Bill Boddice who made his racing debut on a New Hudson. 498 Triumphs finished first and second in each race with a 496 BSA third. The adjudged winner was E. Pelham, whose time in winning the second race was faster than T. Watley's first race win. This event was officially styled the first British road race for standard equipped machines and was run for machines up to 500cc. It was, perhaps, a slight misrepresentation, but it was the first on a British short circuit. War intervened on September 3rd, which was to interrupt the lives of the majority of people. When racing resumed after the war the Clubman's races were to continue where Donington had left off.

Production and Formula 750 Races

With the changing pattern of thought in 1967, it was a foregone conclusion that, eventually, there would be another race for standard machines at the TT. Perhaps memories of Australian Tom Phillis cracking a Bracebridge Street 500 pushrod twin round the Island in 1961 was still very much alive, particularly as he finished third. But it was more than that. The development of the Domiracer had been taking place since 1957, alongside that of the Manx Norton, which plagued the results of the day. Norton could not take their Manx into American racing due to the ban on the overhead camshaft engine, and it was important to develop the twin-cylinder engine which was forming the basis of their normal production output. Doug Hele was the man most involved in the Norton story, so it is an interesting matter of record that he eventually succeeded with the Triumph/BSA group where he failed with Norton. The Domiracer never achieved any greater measure of success although it was raced in the Ulster Grand Prix, and was eventually mothballed when AMC moved the Norton works from Birmingham down to their Plumstead factory in London.

Ray Pickerell on board a 650 Bonneville at Brands Hatch in 1969

Chapter Four Production racing

But the development programme of any serious racing machine depended upon the experience gained at Britain's most prestigous of all races, the TT. The demanding nature of the circuit could not be emulated anywhere else in the world; a circuit of which the late Cal Rayborn said "... man, that's something else!" Most private entrants demanded a race in the Island but the ACU were not convinced in the beginning that such a race would be entirely in the interests of the sport. The Island, after all, had claimed a great number of world class riders and to put the less suitable machines over the tortuous thirty-seven and three-quarter miles circuit would be nothing short of lunacy. On 12th June 1968 the ACU gave way to pressure and the first production race was run under their new rules, over three laps of the circuit, before the Junior race on the same day. The winner was Ray Pickrell riding Paul Dunstall's Dominator Norton at an average speed of 98.13mph. Early mist patches on the Mountain cleared to give an almost perfect day for the race. Split into classes, the smaller capacity machines put up some fine performances, but of course, were not able to match the bigger machines. Ray Knight won the 500 class with a Triumph Daytona at an average speed that put him into fifth place overall. Trevor Burgess, riding a 250 Spanish Ossa, the like of which was similar to that being ridden by that magnificent Spaniard, Santiago Herrero, in the Lightweight race — won the 250 class with a record that would have put him fourth in the 500 class and sixth overall. There were no incidents or accidents throughout both practice and racing and the protests which were expected to be a major part of the aftermath didn't really amount to much.

That first lukewarm tryout was a success and with the fastest lap going to Ray Pickrell at 99.39mph, there was not dynamite made which could shift opinion against the Production TT's right to a place in the programme.

Five Triumph Tridents all set for the Island after being prepared at Norton Triumph International's experimental department at Kitts Green. On the left is Doug Hele, the man who made the threes a force to be reckoned with

Regulations for the 1969 races were tightened up slightly with machines eligible having to be manufactured after 1st January 1964. It was not considered safe to let older machines run which, again, was a sore point to those with Vincents, many of which would have done credit to a 1969 model. Machines had to be standard or comprise only the type of original or optional equipment with which, according to the manufacturer's published specification, similar models of the same year could have been fitted before leaving the factory. Catalogues had to be lodged with the ACU before March 1st 1969. Still there were arguments, but this was only to be expected, and the world's worst problem was in knowing what was standard and what wasn't, on the foreign machines, as few catalogues were ever seen. Honda, at that time, marketed something like one hundred and thirty different models throughout the world with an almost endless interchange of parts, so life in officialdom was not particularly quiet and easy. Optional extra lists, published by the manufacturers in accordance with the regulations, made a mockery of the rules, since the majority could not be obtained by anyone. Even the official dealer entrants were not allowed in on the secrets, in case they somehow managed to beat the official works teams. Although dissatisfaction amongst the competitors was rife, little filtered through the media, who could only report on superb racing, faster and more spectacular than could have been hoped for.

Production racing as a regular class started in Canada as late as 1967, and the sudden foray into racing by manufacturers, particularly the British with the TT in mind, helped no end to satisfy the thirst for this new form of racing over there. The Triumph Trident and BSA three-cylinder models were quick to find their way into welcome hands, but it was still the superlative Triumph Bonnevilles which, though not winning the first Island event, had really made the opposition swelter at short circuit events for almost a twelve month period. Malcolm Uphill really scorched to victory during the three lap event in 1969, marginally ahead of Paul Smart on a Norton Commando. There were really only two riders in the race and the first 100mph lap went to Uphill in glorious weather conditions at a speed of 100.37mph, and an average speed one hundredth of a second inside the average 'ton'. Honda and Ducati won 500 and 250 classes respectively but this time they were not in the hunt for overall honours. The Duke of Edinburgh was present to start the race; royalty returning to honour road racing for the second time in twenty years.

One of the interesting facets of this 1969 event was that, in terms of sheer speed, the Rod Gould machine put in a staggering recorded maximum of 140mph. Paul Smart's machine was the only Norton in the fastest six through the speed trap. And better was to come when the works really got down to the triples.

For the second year running, Malcolm Uphill won the 1970 Production TT (first International race) with an injured foot, so agonising that he could hardly start his machine. On a factory prepared Triumph Trident he snatched a 1.6s victory from Norton's Peter Williams riding a 750 Commando, over the newly extended race distance of five laps. The average speed was down very much because of this new distance, brought about because of the obvious reliability and prowess of a class of racing which had already proved itself. Uphill finished absolutely exhausted due to the hot weather, gruelling concentration due to wet tar on the roads, and his painful foot. Ray Pickrell was third and Tom Dickie fourth, but race positions were not particularly consistent due to the fact that, for a five lap race, riders had to stop for fuel. Tanks had to be of standard capacity. This produced no end of excitement in the pits but, unhappily at the time, spoilt all chances of new records which were very much on the cards. Peter Williams put up the fastest lap at 99.99mph, the identical speed of the race average the previous year. Pickrell's ride had been a disappointment to the crowds as the very likeable Londoner suffered from gearbox trouble, leaving him to coast over the line, gearless, at the end of the race. Hans Otto Butunuth came home in sixth spot on what was obviously a standard BMW.

Formula 750 put in an appearance at the 1971 event, run alongside the Production TT as a bonus for spectators. The rules, drawn up in the February at an AMA/ACU meeting in Cincinatti, were an all-time success with thirty-one riders starting the race which saw new lap records set for the class. Twenty-three year old Tony Jefferies won with a blistering average of 102.85mph and a record lap of 103.21mph. Second was Ray Pickrell and third Peter Williams. Even Peter's average speed was 101.22mph which was witness to the seering pace. Canadian Bert Clark, making his fourth Island appearance, was fourth on the Seeley Yamaha 350. The race was run under National regulations and not under the FIM international banner, which did not recognise the class.

When it came to the International Production machine race Pickrell had his own back, finishing one and a half minutes ahead of Jefferies. In the meantime Jefferies had won the Junior TT on the John Cooper popularised Yamsel, so he could probably give a little to the flying Pickrell. Triumph/BSA took the first three places with Bob Heath third home and there was the familiar sight of the West German made, and ridden, 750 BMW in fourth place. Japanese machines dominated both 500 and 250cc classes. Unlike 1970, when the BSA/Triumph group

Paul Smart was one of the first to chalk up success with the 'threes' in standard production guise. Here he is at Brands Hatch in 1970

Looking almost too standard to be anything more than of initial interest, the legendary 'Slippery Sam', which was so lovingly prepared and later owned by Les Williams

didn't officially enter works machines due to their American commitments, the factories whole-heartedly supported the 1971 attempt to compete against Norton, their major antagonist.

The FIM go-ahead to run Formula 750 as a full International class did not arrive in time for the 1973 races but it didn't matter much to the thousands of fans who flocked to the Island to witness some pretty quick racing. The Saturday Production race was run over four laps and not five, its promotion the year before to the Wednesday of race week being short lived. The expected Norton challenge to the Triumphs fizzled out with broken gearboxes, and poor Tony Jefferies, who had changed to a works Norton for this one race, saw his hopes of success dwindle to nothing as the mighty Ray Pickrell fought on to another victory on the Stan Shenton entered Boyer Trident. In spite of his problems with the Norton box, Peter Williams soldiered on to record his sixth second place in a TT race. Ray Pickrell notched up a record lap on his fourth circuit at 101.61mph but even this was nothing compared to what was to come on the following Thursday.

The problems with gearboxes during the 1972 racing season were due to the length of the overhang on the gearbox mainshaft, between the clutch and gearbox main bearing. It should be remembered that the Norton racing department had only two and a half months to design and produce a Formula 750 machine for the 1972 season due to their decision to participate at the Daytona event. They managed to keep to their deadline and, of course, Phil Read achieved quite a wonderful distinction of a fourth place on a circuit which was not the best available to allow the new machine to be competitive.

As the season progressed the problem of losing teeth off both mainshaft and layshaft constant mesh gears became a major problem. The technicians realised that mainshaft deflection was causing the gears to run out of square so causing a point of loading contact on the teeth. This, together with what they subsequently found to be a wrong gear tooth form, plus the absence of a shock absorber within the gearbox system, brought about the breakages which plagued the Norton team throughout. Whilst the design team worked out a method of eliminating the shaft deflection, the teeth were re-designed and a shock absorber was built into the box. From then on breakages became less frequent.

During practice for the Formula 750 race, Australian Jack Findlay had been clocked through the Highlander speed trap at 154.50mph on the Italian entered 750 Saaid Suzuki, putting up the fastest recorded speed since *Motor Cycle* started their speed trap operation in 1963. In spite of his speed advantage Jack could only manage a third place behind the evergreen Pickrell, who set the Island alight with an average speed of 104.23mph, faster than the 1971 average, and a really beautiful to behold lap record of 105.68mph. His constant shadow, Tony Jefferies, was second holding-off the Findlay Suzuki, the handling of which some viewers likened to riding a pig through a farmyard of spuds! Back to five laps the big bikes had it roughly all their own way, but a gallant performance by Charlie Williams on the Dugdale 350 Yamaha brought him a notable distinction of fifth place. Gearbox troubles continued to plague the Norton team in practice and it was known that special rear wheels had been flown over to the Island which offered some dampening of torque from the chain drive; rather as Royal Enfield used to incorporate in their cush drive. All was in vain, for their brightest hope, Peter Williams, retired with another broken gearbox after having chased the retreating Pickrell for all he was worth. He was lying in second place.

There could be little doubt remaining in anyone's minds that the big bikes were here to stay, and in the October of that year the FIM finally accepted the Anglo/American package of regulations as they stood, being forced to concede the inevitability of an International class for 750cc machines, if not a full world championship series. The latter was, and still is, a dream of many, and there can be little opposition left in practical circles which should delay the matter further. Politics, however, are simply unintelligible, particularly as they are of the International variety, and I doubt that there are many individuals around who know the real reason for the delay.

If 1972 had been a year of despair and despondency, the Norton team arrived at their Douglas headquarters in 1973 in a mood to wipe out the memory of their tragic failure the year before. The prime objective was to win the Formula 750 race, and although the Production race was still considered important it was second in their list of priorities. Probably this was just as well, for Dave Croxford crashed and Peter Williams yet again suffered gearbox failure. It was decided to completely redesign the Norton for 1973 and part of the design criteria was to incorporate an outrigger bearing on the gearbox mainshaft. This was designed into the primary case, and using dished sprockets Norton were able to put the primary loads directly into the bearing and not into an overhanging shaft. The shock absorber was re-located on the engine crankshaft. But while Norton, in their blue, red and white John Player guise, were struggling with their problems, Yamaha were set to announce the latest TZ 700s, producing around the 130bhp mark, which tended to detune the Norton sales team who had just announced new

Perhaps not what to do with a new BMW. Helmut Dahn had many more moments, such as this, in the TT, but at least this is what most do at Ballaugh!

850cc models and a shorter stroked competition engine. News of the TZ700 was bad news indeed, for the 350 watercooled machines had already proved too fast and reliable for comfort. But in the opening Production race it was another win for Shipley's Tony Jefferies, riding the same machine which Ray took to victory the previous year and in 1971 — the legendary Slippery Sam! This machine was built at Meriden in 1970 as one of three for the TT. All other efforts were diverted to the Daytona quest, which left the machines as near standard as they could be, albeit with modifications to the valve gear and camshafts within the permitted rules. The machine which eventually became known as Slippery Sam only failed to finish once, during the 1972 Hutchinson 100, and that was only because Ray Pickrell fell off! It took part in the Bol d'Or and was even sprinted with success.

But Jefferies' win was no easy matter. The kickstart Le Mans-style start was in dry weather which was not to last the race through. The cold and wet race became a nightmare for every rider taking part and it is of great credit to them that few were lured into making many mistakes during the four lap race. Peter Williams was tragically unlucky. Although his machine was slightly slower than the Trident and its handling just about the same — according to Tony Jefferies — Peter had Tony beat until his enforced retirement. He led for the first two laps by a narrow margin and his progress was enough to record the fastest lap at 100.52mph. John Williams on Stan Shenton's Triumph 'three' and Dave Nixon on a similarly entered model proved that privately entered and prepared machines are just as capable of being up with the works teams, by finishing second and third respectively, John riding an impeccable race throughout.

Wednesday was a different story. The new monocoque Formula 750 John Player Norton in the hands of Peter Williams set the Island alight by recording almost the fastest lap the Island had ever seen — 107.27mph and a record average of 105.62. It was victory all the way for the Norton team as Yorkshire's Mick Grant brought the second machine home into second place, with Tony Jefferies third, hot on Mick's tail. Jack Findlay's superfast Suzuki provided an early scare, and lay second for four laps before the gearbox fell apart. The frantic practice pit stops which had been part of the Norton build-up on the Jurby aerodrome, proved of infinite advantage, but when you came down to the nitty-gritty, it was Peter's impeccable riding and skill which won the day on a machine which, it seemed, at long last had shaken the bugs from its bosom.

The emblem on his helmet acknowledging the help given to him by his first sponsor Jim Lee, Mick Grant gets ready to tackle yet another successful race for Kawasaki

The youthful Tony Jefferies whose riding Gary Nixon
found far too strong for him when Gary first came to
England. His hard style earned him few friends in
those days, but his determination carried him
to countless wins and a place in the first British
team

Winner of the 1974 Open Formula Classic — Charles
Mortimer

Alex George aboard a Harley-Davidson in full flight over Ballaugh in 1975

The downhill descent at Bray Hill really sorts the men from the boys, Australian Jack Findlay proves that you don't have to end up on your back wheel

The Production TT looked as though it would never put in another appearance in the Isle of Man, due to the transfer of interest by dealers and entrants to the new and much more glamorous Formula 750 race which was fast becoming the highlight of the week's racing. More so because of the boycott by the accepted star riders of the world championship arena who had previously formed the whole glamour of the event. Before the races for these extra-special 750cc machines had been contemplated, the Production class was well supported and with an attraction very much of its own, due to the factory support which it eventually received. Star riders were contracted to ride, and an increase in capacity to 1000cc allowed the bigger 900 Kawasaki and BMW to enter alongside the 850 Norton, 1000 Laverda and 860 Ducati. The Formula 750 class was specific to that limit and although this capacity had retained total dominance since its inception, this was also due to change during 1974.

After much negotiation *Motor Cycle* and Philip Morris came to the aid of the Production race and it was reinstated as the Marlborough/Motor Cycle event, a race which saw Mick Grant win for the first time, aboard Slippery Sam. Apart from the fact that Peter Williams put in the fastest practice lap for the F750 race at 107.27mph, exactly the same as his race speed the previous year, both his and Dave Croxford's Nortons expired during a race dominated by the 350 watercooled Yamahas. The six lap race was won by Charles Mortimer, with Charlie Williams second and Tony Rutter third, the first big machine home being Percy Tait aboard his '74 Triumph. Only two out of the first nine machines home were 750s and Mick Grant, who had switched to a Boyer Kawasaki for this event, could only manage a seventeenth place and a bronze replica. Charlie Williams proved what the latest breed of 350 Yamahas were all about by lapping at 106.61mph on his last lap, so it appeared, on paper at least, that the only person capable of beating these half sized two strokes was Peter Williams on the Norton — and he had retired on the first lap!

1975 was a good year by Isle of Man standards. The new look ten lap Production TT was won by the legendary 'Slippery Sam' yet again with a record average of 99.60mph, increasing the record lap which the same machine held from the previous year to 102.82mph. This race was run as a two rider affair — the first in the history of the TT — and the Les Williams' Triumph ridden by Scotsman Alex George and the indomitable Dave Croxford, the latter complaining he hadn't had time to stop at a pub! It was an outright win for the Triumph which was followed home by the 250 Yamaha of Charles Mortimer and Billy Guthrie with the Selwyn Griffiths/Dave Williams Triumph in third place. 250cc machines took fourth to ninth places on handicap as well, so you could not really regard the overall results as a firm indication of the going. Of course the big bikes dominated the race which, because it was run as an all class race — the handicap allowed the 250s a lap in hand plus a fourteen second advantage — tended to be a rather unimportant fixture outside the big class itself. Fortunately for the spectator, the classes were started as a mass start instead of the more usual timed starts.

The day before the Production race Mick Grant had set the Island on its toes by breaking the Mike Hailwood lap record by twelve seconds, set in 1967, on the 500 Honda Four, at the same time knocking 6.2s off Peter Williams' big bike record on the opening lap and from a standing start. In spite of this early success, the Kawasaki Three didn't last the race, retiring from a broken chain. This Open Classic race was eventually won by a 350 Yamaha ridden by John Williams who had won the 500 and 250 Production TTs in 1971 and 1972. He completely dominated the race after the Kawasaki had retired, averaging 105.33mph for the six lap race. Percy Tait finished second on an unfamiliar ex Lansivouri Yahama, four minutes in arrears. Grant's lap record lifted the speed to 109.82mph as opposed to Mike's 108.77mph. When Mike claimed that he could lap the Island at 110mph, a year or so before, there were a number of people who found it impossible to believe that it could be done. Mick Grant had gone part of the way in proving that Mike was right!

In looking back at both Production and Formula 750TTs, not to add the later additions in 1975, one cannot help but be surprised at the enormous success of the big bike classes. The original Production class had been demanded by riders as a very necessary break from the continuous ritual of mainland racing, but even their enthusiasm was not enough to provide the display the spectators wanted to see from the much more impressive Formula 750 racers when they at last put in their appearance. Only by dint of hard work did the production riders keep their own race on the cards. Not surprisingly, the racers claimed much of the glamour, and since few riders could afford to race two machines, they had to choose between one or the other. That the Production class has survived is a great tribute to both riders and entrants, who would not relinquish their right to race in the magic Isle of Man, where the now legendary lap at a ton is still as highly prized an achievement as it ever was before. That the roads have improved almost beyond recognition along with the vast improvement in machine performance is not reason enough to discount a 100mph lap as being unworthy of note. Of all the world's race circuits, the Isle of Man Mountain course is the toughest and it requires a totally different mental approach to all others. I believe it safe to add that there will never be another like it, for the standards of safety required of modern circuits are quite beyond comprehension when compared to the 37¾ mile TT course. The fact that it survives the political pressure to have it closed is witness to the sheer determination of the riders themselves to have the Island kept open for their own enjoyment. While it is still viable to run a TT fortnight it will be the first to resist all pressures to change and the last to succumb. It is fair to say that wherever possible, safety is of the most supreme importance, but it remains a circuit where men are men, and where the beer slowly improves the longer you stay!

5 Daytona and the 200
Imola and the other 200

Daytona is as perfect a place as you could wish to find anywhere in the world unless, of course, you have unlimited financial resources. Perhaps it smacks too much of the tourist spot for a nice sojourn, but this one factor alone, perhaps, adds as much to the enjoyment of the masses as the annual classic motorcycle races — the Daytona 200. Crowds pour into the Florida speed capital from all over the world. Daytona was once described as a city where the smell of racing fuel is as common and as pleasing to the inhabitants as the scent of tropical flowers. I am not so sure I agree with this sentiment entirely since Daytona can be decidedly chilly at the beginning of March and I have yet to smell the scent of flowers, perhaps due to nasal congestion after a British winter. In any case there is a strict difference between the beach, with its long line of motels, the city with its huge river meandering through, and the circuit itself, which is nothing like either. You can be in one place without even knowing that the other exists, such is the expanse which makes the appeal of Daytona as varied as you need to make it. The time taken to travel between all three demands motorised transport, and it is always a wise precaution to find out exactly where that luxury motel is before you decide that you can do without it — the vehicle that is: Vagrancy is discouraged!

Perhaps the description was penned during the days when the golden sands, which stretch in each direction as far as the eye can see, were used for the original speed racing. Twenty miles of solid sand five hundred foot wide at low tide borders the warm Atlantic so it is little wonder that they were in use as early as February 1903. Men like Henry Seagrave and Malcolm Campbell made their reputations, if not their knighthoods, on the sands; the latter lifting the world absolute record to 276.80mph before being beckoned away by the lure of the Bonneville Salt Flats at Utah for the world records to come. Motorcycles first put in an appearance in 1904 when Glen Curtiss became the first to clock 60mph, a much different scene to today where the only vehicles to use the beach are Cadillacs and the like restricted to 10mph. Curtiss became the fastest man in the world in 1908 when he set a record of 136mph on a vee 8 engined motorcycle, based upon an aero engine. Even in those days the almost unbelievable size and scope of technology and futurism of the American scene made Europe look slightly drab and unviting! In 1949 Norton 'Manx' machines were first and second in the Amateur race, and first, second and third in the Professional. The machines were standard racing models, part of the normal export to North America, but specially prepared by Francis Beart.

With a background of doom and despondency, the United States economy slumped with the Wall Street Crash of 1929. Jobs were hard to come by with few people able to jingle spare dimes or quarters in the linings of their depleted pockets. The motor and motorcycle industry was at a very low ebb indeed, but racing had to continue and so it did, albeit on a reduced and altered scale. The American Motorcycle Association sat down and deliberated over some new plans to limit competition to what were essentially street machines. Machines were based upon the concept of production models and this meant that you rode your machine to a meeting, removed the non-essentials and then got on with the job of racing. If you were lucky you won a two-dollar medal, ten feet of chain or a couple of spark plugs.

History suggests that four men met in a motorcycle shop in Savannah and talked over the idea of bringing together this new form of racing, and the groups which ran them, for an event that would be recognised nationally. They arranged a deal with the city of Savannah for the use of the old Vanderbilt Cup Course and on April 26th 1932 put on the first two hundred mile race. It was a meagre beginning but it set the scene for bigger and better things to come. The organisers sweated and toiled to improve the spectator potential and the race was moved

It was often a question of taking your bike to the event and then racing it. At least you had no trouble with the guard rail!

from Savannah to Jacksonville, back to Savannah and eventually, in 1937, to Daytona Beach, to the golden sands that were fast gaining an impressive reputation as the years unfolded. This first two hundred miler was won by Ed Kretz on an Indian. A couple of single cylinder Nortons provided the only variation to the whole mass of Milwaukee and Springfield flatheads. A Norton came second and a Harley Davidson third. Canadian Bill Matthews broke the United States monopoly in 1941, when he won for Norton.

The Daytona Beach circuit measured 3.2 miles in length and incorporated both sand and tarmac. Rather like the old Avus circuit in Germany, it was basically two straights and two corners. Until 1960 this layout played host to the 200, although beach modifications meant moving the site to a slightly longer course in 1948, which measured a mile longer. This 1948 race was won by Floyd Emde whose two sons are very much following in father's footsteps. In fact Don won the 1972 Daytona 200 on a 350 Yamaha.

In February of 1959 the first car meeting was run on the new Daytona speed bowl and the 200 was moved there in 1961, onto the two mile circuit for the first time, preceded by the not too popular United States Motor Cycle Club's so-called Grand Prix. The two types of racing clashed as much as did the American politics which surrounded them, there being a very firm split between the out-and-out European type of racer and the very much production based American machines which had provided the whole concept of stateside racing from the earlier charter. The European-styled organisation, Motorcyle International Committee of United States, was affiliated to the Federation Internationale Motorcycliste, as they believed that motorcycle racing was an international sport. AMA, at that time, were quite happy with what they had and saw little if no benefit in any change. They could manage quite successfully without any outside interferance or influence and firmly intended to keep it that way. Who could blame them? The American continent was quite big enough and prosperous enough to support itself and any infiltration from countries outside the immediate environment was looked upon as unnecessary and pointless. We know now that there is a vast benefit in international competition at any level and I think that this outside influence has helped no end in tangible benefits within America as a whole. This is not to say that our system was better than theirs, for history has shown that the combination of the two has succeeded, where either one or the other would have failed miserably.

In 1961 Southampton rider Tony Godfrey was the first of Britain's successful riders to cross the Atlantic to Daytona, where he won the 125 mile race on Tommy Robb's Matchless G50, loaned by Geoff Monty for the occasion. Tony was notorious for not having machines! The races were repeated from 1962 to 1965 and it is a matter of record that Japan took a serious interest for the first time in 1962, a race being won by Takahashi on a works Honda. Don Vesco took the 250cc rotary valve works Yamaha to victory in 1963 where he resoundly thrashed the Manx Nortons and G50s, again in a race that should, by FIM standards, have shown a 350cc lower limit! American Lance Weil finished second — you will doubtless recall his face on British circuits seven or eight years ago when he rode an 883 Harley Davidson — and Canadian Roger Beaumont was third.

Mike Hailwood took the mighty Italian MV Augusta to Daytona for the first time in 1964 and won. What the record books do not readily reveal is that he had one heck of a scrap with the Argentinian, Benedicto Calderalla, on a seven year old Gilera, mothballed since Gilera's retirement from road racing. Calderalla's first European outing was at Imola during the next month, where he beat the Italian Remo Venturi, setting race and lap records. He went on to break the lap record at Vallelunga and San Remo before returning to obscurity. But this first event opened the eyes of the American public, if only marginally, to the fact that European racing did exist and had much to offer. It was the first real breakthrough. Mike repeated the lesson in 1965, winning from Parriott and Beaumont, enhancing his own particular reputation in the United States, which was to stand him in good stead during future years. His father had property in Nassau which no doubt helped his local reputation in any case, but I have a distinct feeling that Mike's reappearance in later years helped a lot in founding the type of racing that we now know. Although Tony won the race in 1961 it was Mike that the sparse crowd came to see. He retired with magneto failure in the 500 class but won the 250 race on Provini's 1957 Mondial, finishing ahead of Moto Kitano and the Honda Four which finished fifth in the 1960 Lightweight TT. European machines dominated the 500 race, in which Bud Parriott came second on a Norton and Bob Burnett third on a G50. Tony won about £700 but complained that his net figure, after deduction of his travelling expenses and hotel bill, was considerably less.

During that particular race week of 1964 Mike also smashed the late Bob McIntyre's world one hour record, but few saw it happen. The Speedbowl was empty as Mike hurled the 500 MV round its wide open spaces; empty, that is, apart from those of us who were privileged to watch.

1964 also saw the 200 mile race moved to the 3.81 mile track which utilised both speedbowl and inner circuit. During the next six years Triumph were the only motorcycle to split the Harley-Davidson domination

"Who needs four wheels anyway?" The legendary Mike Hailwood was lured away from motor racing to race a works BSA at Daytona in 1971

with Buddy Elmore in 1966 and Gary Nixon in 1967. Roger Reimann clinched two consecutive wins in 1964 and 1965, a feat repeated by Cal Rayborn in 1968 and 1969.

It is worthwhile to digress slightly at this point since the two types of racing were coming together on the same circuit and at the same time. Daytona had become a legend and the American motorcycle scene had been broken into by Europeans, albeit with a lot of effort, for the first time in 1961, even though the Americans didn't generally approve. English tuners and technicians, notably Francis Beart and Steve Lancefield, had been to the beach course to look after Norton interests, but we are now talking about a permanent site for a race which had a lot to offer, if only the public could be made aware of the facilities and spectacle available. Motorcycling in the United States was a popular sport and a convenient mode of transport and pleasure. The wide open spaces, lacking in Europe, lent themselves to the social angle, but rather as in this country, it had long suffered a poor reputation inflicted upon it by the unruly elements of a lower-class society who found an outlet in motorcycles. Movie pictures didn't help very much and the image was deteriorating rather than the reverse. Cafe racing existed both in Europe and America where, even today, the dubiously clad coffee bar cowboy continues to heap scorn upon the heads of the motorcycling movement as a whole.

I can remember sitting in Bill France's office at Daytona one March, discussing the poor spectator attendance. He claimed that he wan't too perturbed at that stage as he was convinced that motorcycling was a basically new sport to the American people, to which they would come when it became more founded. His foresight has been proved correct during the ensuing years but I wonder how many of us in Europe would have stuck so religiously to such ideals, particularly in view of the obvious earlier disappointments and the failure of the United States Grand Prix to attract hardly anyone. The question is almost rhetorical: Bill France is Daytona (as well as Talledega) so the question is almost fundamental. Although totally a car man he was also well aware of the growing impetus of the motorcycling movement which he did much to encourage at a time when there was little encouragement around. The Daytona circuit was built in 1958/59 at a reported cost of well over $3,000,000, and whereas it would be easy to sit back and gloat over the popularity of the place now, it was probably a far different risk in those days. Ten years later, Bill (middle name Getty) created a similar project in Alabama — Talledega. It was destined to be faster and smoother than Daytona with a 2.6 mile outer oval and an inner road circuit of 4 miles as compared to the 3.81 of Daytona. This circuit was to provide the second site for a major new league race and, with it, encouragement for manufacturers and industry to get stuck into major programmes of development. The agreement reached between AMA and FIM in 1970 also provided a basis for a new concept to racing which was about to invade Europe.

This agreement was a little different to that of twenty years before when the late Graham Walker approached the AMA to ask whether an Englishman could ride in their unique sand-cum-road race. The answer was in the affirmative but when Bob Foster wanted to enter it appeared that he had to qualify in their smaller events, so that was officially that.

From 1966 British riders had raced at the Daytona 200 meeting, going via Canada to obtain their licence or straight to the AMA. The FIM, of which we in England were of a corporate body (and still are, come to that), would only recognise MICUS as representative of the American rider, the body which had sanctioned the Grand Prix races from 1961. The type of racing that the American public wanted to see was that run by AMA and since this body was not recognised by the FIM, there was no chance that European riders would be allowed to compete with their FIM licence. If you think it confusing now, you should have been around at the time when the whole rigmarole was under lengthy and often ill-conceived debate! There was even some talk within European circles of riders who took part losing their FIM licences, but little came of it in the end. All that it did was to make some of our better riders emigrate to the United States where their undisputed talent put them in the money market. Some came back when they discovered that National Health was non existent and later Vietnam made the call of Britain a little more vociferous! Racing was crying out for the type of exchange which would advance the sport, and there was no doubt in anyone's mind that the future would be far rosier by opening up that elusive trans-Atlantic link. That it succeeded is obvious to all but the story is probably best told in the chapter on Match Race Magic.

On March 15th 1970 the Triumph and BSA 'threes' were entered from this country with the great Mike Hailwood on BSA. The beautifully prepared machines were a striking contrast to the heavier and uglier American versions which Pete Colman and Danny Macias engineered, and it was obvious from the first practice period that the British engineering and preparation by Doug Hele was as envied as the Hailwood reputation. Honda had entered the fray with ex-works teamsters Tommy Robb and Ralph Bryans, both of them rather diminutive

Ulstermen for the heavy CB750. Cal Rayborn was not very optimistic about his chances on the Harley-Davidson which had won the two previous years. A rule change had been forced through AMA congress which had suddenly outdated his successful side-valve Harley-Davidson — it was supposed that Triumph BSA Incorporated had been behind this very much political move — and he had to go into the big race on a very new and completely untried Milwaukee machine. The rulebook limited 750cc engines to side-valves, since the bigger capacity was reckoned to be equated to the smaller ohv and ohc engines by this restriction. When Canadian Bill Matthews won the 1950 race on a production Manx Norton — his second win which had been interrupted by war years — an immediate ban on them was imposed. Authorities were concerned that the Norton had developed outside the scope of the competition, even though it was only two thirds the size of the American machines. I wonder how they would reconcile today's situation where, apart from a rather elevated facsimile of a production engine and gearbox unit, the rest of the machine is not recognisable as a street model! At least you could then buy a Manx Norton complete.

Perhaps, in the event, poetic justice prevailed and Dick Mann won on yet another works Honda CB750. Ten seconds behind came Eugene Romero on a USA Triumph Trident and third was Don Castro, similarly mounted. The race was a turning point in Anglo/American relations and another offshoot was to make a much firmer impression into the traditional drab British scene. The Americans didn't allow all black leathers; perhaps they didn't suffer from oil-stained hands or have to crawl around in the paddock. Because of this ruling both Mike and Percy Tait had new leathers flown out to them. Mike's, I remember, were black, white and red, while Percy's were just red and black, a class distinction if ever there was one! Although Mike was second fastest in practice, his BSA suffered from misfiring and he retired after ten laps of the race with a broken valve. English expatriate Ron Grant, who was due to ride the 500 Suzuki, had been delighted with the prospect of beating Mike before the race. In fact he had never managed to get near him on British circuits, his greatest ambition. Ron passed Mike on lap ten and shot into the lead with a big grin on his face which lasted until he ran out of fuel and seized solid! Apart from Mann, all the other Hondas went out with camshaft chain breakages. Romero's second place was sufficient to send the Triumph BSA executives back to England in the frame of mind to win next year. If the race had lasted just that little big longer Romero would have overtaken Dick Mann. But as Kipling said ... If!

I have always found it easy to be enthusiastic at Daytona, thousands of miles away from the reality of a city office, the drudgery of beating the rush-hour traffic and the cold, driving rain. Daytona, under these circumstances is unreal; a mirage amongst the myriad discomforts of an English winter. You can come back full of bright and colourful ideas with the answers to the world's problems at your fingertips but to expect the condition to last is a cat of a different colour.

Last it did, and in 1971 the British winter was cast aside on March 14th. Hailwood had been signed for BSA but this time for BSA Incorporated of New Jersey, adding strength to the team of Dave Aldana, Jim Rice and Dick Mann. In the four man Triumph team were Gene Romero, Gary Nixon, Don Castro and Tom Rockwood. The race was yet another disappointment for Mike the Bike, who again suffered machine failure, and for the British works entry Paul Smart, whose Triumph led the field from the start to the forty-second lap, only to have it go onto two cylinders with smoke pouring from the third. "Buggsy" Mann won for BSA with "Burrito" Romero second on Triumph and Don Emde third, a complete walk-over for the British threes which left a trail of devastation behind them. The pace had been hot; too hot for Gary Fisher's privately entered Honda which had led for four laps before his engine blew. It was a supreme race for this twenty year old who had carried Honda laurels at this one early stage of the race. Cal Rayborn retired on the first lap with gearbox problems, spending a lengthy time in the pits trying to replace parts. The 500 Suzukis of Jody Nicholas, Art Baumann and New Zealander Geoff Parry were not in the running, and although Jim Odom brought a 350 Yamaha into fifth place, smaller machines were generally outpaced by the bigger mounts. How times were to change!

MV Agusta did not take part in the 1972 races as they had earlier threatened. Their 750 four cylinder machine had suffered handling problems which, combined with a disappointing lack of power, had led to their withdrawal at an early stage of intent. The biggest tragedy was to hit British hopes — BSA and Triumph pulled out of racing at a time when the scene had been set for their success both on the racing circuits of the world and commercially. They left a couple of private machines. Norton Villiers sent out their two new 750 racers for Phil Read and Peter Williams and both Suzuki and Kawasaki had their new 750 projectiles off the drawing board and onto the circuit, a significant development for the seriously minded Japanese. America's greatest road race was fast becoming the world's greatest, overshadowing the Isle of Man Tourist Trophy by the sheer glamour of men

Water cooled 750 Suzuki triples signalled a new era in road racing when they made their debut at Daytona in 1972. At that time they were the first road racing motorcycles to be officially timed at over 170mph — Art Baumann touched 172.75mph along the front straight during practice

H2R Kawasaki. Dry weight 338lb. 100bhp at 9,000rpm. The power unit around which sat the 1973 riders; DuHamel, Baumann, Nixon and Carr

and machines. True, there was the sunshine as well, which did quite a bit to help. Tyre problems and mechanical failures produced a bit of an anti-climax and it was left to the 350 Yamahas to fill the first three places. Don Emde won £5,000 in front of a record 46,000 people and couldn't believe it had happened. The 750cc machines had fallen like nine-pins, the first to finish being the comparatively underpowered Norton of Phil Read, who rode a well judged race to come home fourth. Engine and gearbox troubles plagued Kawasaki; clutch and flat tyres the Suzuki squad. The problem of taming the 110bhp monsters was becoming a problem, the power output being far too great for component parts, including frame, tyres and, of course, the engine itself. It was a question of going flat-out from the start. You couldn't sit back and expect your competitors to break down, you had to ride the race from the start and just trust to luck. Planning tactics was just pointless. Speeds had rocketed and it became a problem hanging onto your machine under acceleration and the high speeds on the bowl. It wasn't so much a case of steering the bike as pointing it in the right direction. Nine riders had led the race and it was the first time that a two-stroke had won the 200. Don's father Floyd had won the event himself way back in '48 so there was double reason for celebration.

Racing had taken the inevitable step once again. The rule book, aimed at providing racing for 'street' machines, was gradually being expanded, within the context of the rules admittedly, but the fact remained that the machines now putting in an appearance were almost true racers based upon a standard road machine engine. The design of the engine was for a racer, detuned for a road bike; the type which one found in the shop window was a poor comparison to the one on the track. Perhaps this was no bad thing.

New and even greater enthusiasm welcomed the 1973 event with the announcement of the 117bhp, 183mph Suzukis which were to make their debut at Daytona on March 11th. British hopes of achieving a win had been diminished with the BSA Triumph withdrawal and it now became a case of if you can't beat 'em, join 'em; the them in this case being the resurgent Japanese motorcycle titans. Their interest in the development of the new era of big bikes was there for all to see; engineered, perhaps within the technical and democratic committees of the AMA, who knows, but a welcome sight nevertheless. The prize money and prestige which Daytona attracted was enormous and the potential sales within the United States market balanced on a keen knife-edge of competition, the pendulum of success or failure tipping it either one way or the other. In line with the trend for bigger, better and quicker machines Kawasaki and even Honda were marketing machines within the 900cc bracket and, of course, Harley-Davidson had continued their magnificent range of running-board machinery into the seventies.

Lining up in front of the main grandstand are, left to right; DuHamel, Nixon and Smart

Thirty works machines were entered for the '73 races, with teams fielding strength in numbers as well as in technical ability. Kawasaki were offering a bonus of £8000 to anyone, providing they rode a Kawasaki into first position, a sentiment which strongly favoured the Bob Hansen 'works' Kawasaki team. I have two minds as to whether or not this was a sensible bonus. It is one thing to give good prize money but yet another to invite someone to stick their neck out for such a large sum. But then the sport was never designed for the weak at heart!

The Kawasaki H2R machines were down on power to the new water-cooled Suzukis, which already had the reputation of being the most powerful motorcycles in the world following tests in Japan during the winter months. Yvon 'Superfrog' DuHamel and Art 'the Dart' Baumann were in no mood for compromise and were out to win, particularly in view of the added incentive from Kawasaki. Gary Nixon and Cliff Carr were also mounted on the green meanies while Paul Smart had changed camps to Suzuki after a disappointing haggle with Bob Hansen. Yamaha had added water-cooling to the 350s which now also sported a six speed gearbox, a combination which was enough to win, but few thought it really possible in view of the might of the rest of the field. Jarno Saarinen, Europe's world-beater, riding his first race in America and a perfectly judged one at that, won the race. He was always fast enough to be in contention but allowed the Superbikes to self destruct in front of him. If they had kept going there was no way that the small Yamaha could have beaten the big bikes, especially on paper, where the Suzuki and Kawasaki camps led the top seven qualifiers for the race. Both DuHamel and Baumann slid off onto the pavement, together, and although they remounted it was one of those silly incidents which ought never to have happened. Nixon holed a piston and Smart suffered ignition problems, apart from being rammed at the start, an ignominy which had almost ruined Ron Grant's racing career a year or so before. Geoff Parry also lacked enough sparks to finish, Jack Findlay seized, and Ron Grant's chain broke. Out of the twelve big bikes entered from the Japanese two-stroke camps only one survived — Don Emde, in fifth place. Yamaha were jubilant. Australian team manager Kel Carruthers finished second and Jim Evans third, making it a clean sweep for Yamaha. While they celebrated, the mocking bird sang over the scattered debris of those all too powerful projectiles which couldn't quite manage to stay in one piece long enough.

A reported crowd of 61,000 watched this race, a further vindication of the faith and effort put into the promotion of racing at Daytona and of the type of racing which had struggled through the harder times. Big bike racing was what the public came to watch, whether or not the big bike was a mouse that roared. On

The fastest rider in practice has never won the 200. A case in point for Paul Smart

Don Emde won £5,000 and couldn't believe it had happened

Pit stops are crucial in long distance American events. Here the Suzuki team practice a stop with Ron Grant's 750 triple in 1972

Start of the world's most important race in 1973. Gary Nixon (9), Art Baumann (30), Masahiro Wada (33) and Yvon DuHamel (17) dominate on the factory Kawasaki triples

this grand international scale it mattered little that a 350 won; the fact that spectators could witness such a superb variety of machinery was enough to enrapture them throughout the day and the preceding week of practice and qualifying.

Yamaha returned to victory in 1974 with the TZ700, referred to at the time as the TZ750 by some journalists. But they had shrugged off the small capacity machine cloak and produced one twice the size with twice the cylinders. This was to be its very first race outing and multi-world champion Giacomo Agostini was set to ride it for the first time following his change-over from the MV Agusta factory. Paul Smart qualified fastest, yet again, but the Daytona fable that the fastest qualifier never wins proved to be true once more. In 90 degrees of heat, the hottest for years, the big bikes proved themselves at long last, Giacomo lifting the race average to a new record but over the reduced length of 47 laps (170 miles) to conserve fuel in the oil crisis which had hit the world's economy. A chicane had been added in 1973 and the length of the circuit marginally increased as a result. Kenny Roberts coasted into second place with the Kawasaki of Hurley Wilvert, ex-team mechanic, third. Giacomo pocketed a record purse of £6,500 and the glory of winning his first major race with the new Yamaha. Kenny was disappointed to finish second, a position he was to fill again later in the year at Imola. Paul Smart eventually finished ninth in spite of losing two laps when his quick fuel filler refused to operate. Instead of three or four seconds it took as many minutes.

One thing about the AMA rule book is that it endeavours to stop the potential development of the super racers by stating that any machine can be bought after the race for 5000 dollars. Hopefully, this is designed to create a situation of equality; the fact that it doesn't is a matter of history! Patrick Pons slapped his cash onto the table and looked towards taking Agostini's Yamaha away with him, a repetition of an earlier episode at Ontario which almost lost Triumph/BSA one of their 'threes'. No wonder Yamaha put a high price on their machines from then on! Neither got the machine they were after but then common sense prevailed in the end.

Preceding the races themselves, Gene Romero captured the world one hour record which had remained dormant for ten years. The new record of 150.66mph on the 750 was yet another example of Yamaha domination. Three Daytona 200 wins in as many years, two of them with 350 machines, plus the world record; that was a feat that would take some beating. But even bigger and better things were to come.

You can read their names, but left to right are Araoka, Smart, Nixon, Carr, Sheene and Merv Wright

Master mind behind the Yamaha success in America is the 1969 World 250 Champion, Kel Carruthers. He learnt his trade the hard way — obviously he has come a long way since his Honda 4 days in Australia

Never out of the hunt on flat track and road courses is Gene Romero

In the sun of Daytona Kenny Roberts is as happy as he is anywhere else — out front!

Viewed by American riders as the world's greatest road racer, Cal Rayborn always put in some stirling performances but never won the AMA title. He did win Daytona in 1968 and 1969

Canadian Stever Baker who has laid claim to honour in 1976

The shear brutish power-house of the 750 Yamaha

Yamaha supremacy at Daytona in 1975 was no suprise to anyone, but the eventual results, as always, were beyond even informed guesswork. As Caldarella came, so did Cecotto, who stormed to a fine third place behind Romero and Canadian Steve Baker. Romero's handling of the mighty TZ750 Yamaha was magnificent and a firm support to his improving reputation as a works Yamaha rider. Yamaha, in fact, took the first sixteen places, with Romero's win his first at Daytona after being bridesmaid on no less than three previous occasions. His winning speed was also the fastest ever recorded for the race. With all eyes beforehand centred on the return battle between Agostini and Roberts — remember that Ago had twice beaten Roberts in their two previous encounters — few would have granted that any other rider would stand a chance, but as is so often the case when speeds start reaching these lofty proportions mechanical failures have to be accepted increasingly more so in such long tiring races when little opportunity presents itself for any relaxation of man or machine. It came as no great surprise when Roberts' Yamaha hit clutch trouble. He was obviously out to decimate the opposition and from his progress there was really only one man in the race. Agostini soldiered on but could only manage a fourth place, being overtaken four laps from the end by a determined and speedy Cecotto. One wonders if Agostini knew just how close Cecotto really was, but once past there was no way that Ago could get into the winner's circle. West Coast rider Steve McLoughlin, whose father was himself a leading figure in the early '60s political intrigues within MICUS, found himself in the lead for ten laps until he lost concentration and fell off. Steve Baker also had the lead until he was overhauled by Romero. Lansivouri, too, had his moments of success until he stepped off after a meteoric ride which, could he but have stayed aboard, might have given him a well deserved win. At the final curtain it was Romero's race, cheque and trophy. Steve Baker remained to finish second on the Canadian entered Yamaha and with Cecotto and Agostini taking third and fourth places, Warren Willing finished fifth and a plucky McLoughlin sixth, after dusting himself off after his fall.

A Production race was introduced for the first time at the '200' on the Friday afternoon, to be run over ten laps. This was won by Dave Aldana on a Yoshimura 900 Kawasaki. In the 100 mile Junior race Yamaha also dominated not only the entry but also the results as well, taking the first eighteen places. The race was won by Gary Blackman at 102.10mph.

To me Daytona is that something extra special. It comes at the time of year most suitable for a big promotion and marks the first International event of the year. That it is held in the warmth of Florida is an additional atrraction, particularly for a European who by March has had more than his fair share of winter. I have been to Daytona quite a number of times and have yet to get fed up with the wheels touching down at Miami or Jacksonville. From Miami it is a drive up the turnpike if you're in a hurry; if you're not you can take the scenic route along the sand dunes or the rather less interesting main road. The weather is invariably warm or hot. If it's raining it's still either warm or hot; the sort of rain which is a marked relief after what we in England have been used to for the previous three months.

Other events may try to emulate Daytona but none will succeed in surpassing what must rank as the greatest of the world's races.

Daytona 200 Results

1937	Ed Kretz	Indian	73.34mph
1938	Ben Campanele	H–D	73.99mph
1939	Ben Campanele	H–D	76.68mph
1940	Babe Tancrede	H–D	75.11mph
1941	Billy Matthews	Norton	78.08mph
1947	John Spiegelhoff	Indian	77.14mph
1948	Floyd Emde	Indian	74.01mph
1949	Dick Klamfoth	Norton	86.42mph
1950	Billy Matthews	Norton	88.55mph
1951	Dick Klamfoth	Norton	92.81mph
1952	Dick Klamfoth	Norton	87.71mph
1953	Paul Goldsmith	H–D	94.25mph
1954	Bobby Hill	BSA	94.24mph
1955	Brad Andres	H–D	94.57mph
1956	John Gibson	H–D	94.21mph
1957	Joe Leonnard	H–D	98.52mph

1958	Joe Leonnard	H–D	99.86mph
1959	Brad Andres	H–D	98.70mph
1960	Brad Andres	H–D	98.06mph
1961	Roger Reimann	H–D	69.250mph
1962	Don Burnett	Triumph	71.981mph
1963	Ralph White	H–D	77.678mph
1964	Roger Reimann	H–D	94.833mph
1965	Roger Reimann	H–D	90.041mph
1966	Buddy Elmore	Triumph	96.582mph
1967	Gary Nixon	Triumph	98.227mph
1968	Cal Rayborn	H–D	101.290mph
1969	Cal Rayborn	H–D	100.882mph
1970	Dick Mann	Honda	102.690mph
1971	Dick Mann	BSA	104.737mph
1972	Don Emde	Yamaha	103.358mph
1973	Jarno Saarinen	Yamaha	98.178mph
1974	Giacomo Agostini	Yamaha	105.010mph
1975	Eugene Romero	Yamaha	106.450mph

IMOLA AND THAT OTHER '200'

The advent of an Americanised race at Imola in 1972 was not as surprising as it might have seemed at the time. It was local knowledge that the Italians were keen to surpass all other European organisers with this new form of event and even gave forewarning of their interest in 1971, when they staged a production race which Augusto Brettoni won on a Laverda. Monza had already been the scene of a 500 kilometre race for production machines and there was little doubt that the Moto Club Santerno, who organised that initial flourish at Imola, were keen and enthusiastic to put on the finest event in Europe for this latest craze of big bike racing. They had plenty of experience to back them. Long gone were the days of the almost maniacal approach to scooter rallies, racing and long distance events; and the very much Italian Catholic distaste for a lady riding straddled across a pillion had almost, but not quite, disappeared. The Match Races had proved an enormous success in England, and so, too, had the new ACU International at Silverstone, which was destined to become bigger and better than any previous event held there, with the additional advantage of a five year lapse of motorcycle racing on the Northants circuit. The BSA and Triumph threes had been homolgated for Formula 750 racing and John Cooper had successfully beaten the 500 MV Agusta of Giacomo Agostini; first after a breathtaking race in front of a record Mallory Park Race of the Year crowd; secondly at Brands Hatch in the October of that incredible 1971. Then he went on to win at Ontario on the very same machine, the BSA three which, John claimed, was the only really competitive machine that he had ever ridden.

With such a background, the time was ripe for another big meeting, which the world witnessed on the Dino Ferrari circuit at Imola on April 23rd 1972. Motorcycling will long remember that first meeting for it was a lesson in how enthusiasm overrides all problems — although it did create others. Paul Smart will also remember that meeting for this was the first of his really big money wins at a time when he was disappointingly let down by Triumph, who could not supply him with a machine at the last minute. Ducati, too, will remember that meeting as the one they least expected to win. It was a huge winner for Italy in the best traditions of sport, for not only did they create a European 200 for the first time, but they also provided prize money to suit the occasion — some £20,000 of it. Most of the Italian factories turned out in force for the first time since the late 'fifties. MV Agusta produced the 743 transverse four racer for one of its few appearances, and the Linto Tonti-designed Moto Guzzis were out in force, following their only previous success of fifteen world records in 1969, breaking a twelve year spell of indifference to racing. These race kitted sports 750 vee twin models finished tenth and eleventh, an unusual sight with cylinders sticking out sideways.

On his 29th birthday, and a couple of months after anulling his record breaking liaison with Triumph in favour of a contract with Team Hansen in California, Paul Smart rode a vee-twin 84bhp 750 Ducati into first place, closely followed by ex Grand Prix Ducati rider Bruno Spaggiari. It was a result which few had anticipated, least of all Paul and Bruno who were delighted to prove so invincible at this first event. So delighted were Ducati that they gave Paul the winning machine to go with his cheque for around £4,500. It was not a happy occasion for the MV Agusta factory because their hastily prepared machine — hasty, that is, for MV — lost revs and eventually fell by the wayside. Theirs was not the tale of success to which they had become very much accustomed over the years, but the constant battle to produce a quicker world championship machine in face of the Yamaha opposition, little time had been left to develop the 750 machine, a machine which was severely handicapped due to the fact that it had to use the standard shaft-drive with which the production models were fitted. Giacomo Agostini didn't exactly hang around and equalled the fastest lap at over 100mph, shared with the two Ducatis. So, for Paul, Fredmano Spairani's last-minute offer of a machine had been gold.

Shell had taken on the sponsorship of the first 200 in 1972 which the Italians had been happy to call the Daytona of Europe. No less than twenty-one works' riders had been listed, a foretaste of things to come, but the most encouraging aspect was the crowd which was reported as being in excess of 70,000, and the interest of Italian Television Network who covered the meeting live.

Shell continued their sponsorship into 1973 but were joined by AGV Helmets and the local ceramics firm of Santerno Ceramica. The prize fund was increased to £27,000 and a guaranteed sum paid to each rider to assist with his expenses. The race was split into two legs, each of 100 miles, more like Talledega and Ontario than the Daytona event it was meant to emulate. American riders joined in force for the first time but it was the late Jarno Saarinen, killed at Monza a short month later, who shattered the galaxy of riders. Incredibly, the heavy and cumbersome desmodromic Ducati was again second, with Spaggiari on board, while Villa repeated his first year position by finishing third. Teuvo Lansivouri was fourth and Kel Carruthers, making his first European appearance since he left for the States in 1970, finished fifth, ahead of Jack Findlay on the Saaid Suzuki. This event

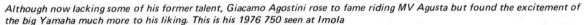

Although now lacking some of his former talent, Giacamo Agostini rose to fame riding MV Agusta but found the excitement of the big Yamaha much more to his liking. This is his 1976 750 seen at Imola

also marked Nortons first foray into European racing and saw the first appearance in Europe of the 750 Kawasaki threes in the hands of DuHamel, Baumann and Nixon. By 1974 the race was well established, although Shell had reluctantly to withdraw their support due to the energy crisis, which was incompatible with large scale sponsorship. SIM Prefabbricati stepped in, which made it an all-Italian affair for the first time. Two new chicanes were introduced in an endeavour to reduce the speeds, forced through by the Italian Federation as a direct result of Saarinen's death during the Monza accident, which had also robbed Italy of one of its idols, Renzo Passolini. The arrival of the Americans in force indicated the new status of the event, particularly as American Champion Kenny Roberts was over for the first time. Giacomo Agostini, although he had ridden the 750 MV during the previous two events, had switched camps, and now joined Yamaha so that he could be more competitive in this big bike class; and since he had already won the prestigous Daytona meeting he was keen to retain his record, particularly in view of his poor showing on the 500 Yamaha during the earlier Italian championship events at Misano and Modena.

The FIM struck just before Imola and the TZ700 was ruled ineligible. The Italians, after a short flurry, chose to ignore the ban by running the event as a straight 750cc race rather than to Formula 750 rules and the two Yamaha teams were allowed to race on, forfeiting the FIM points which were otherwise to have resulted from the competition. It is a matter of record that Ago won for the second time in two successive 750 rides but the writing was very much on the wall. Teppi Lansivouri was fastest in practice, ahead of Ago and Barry Sheene, while Roberts trailed in fourth place ahead of the indomitable Walter Villa. On race day the torrid heat raised the race to scorching heights when Roberts shot into a lead which he steadily increased lap by lap. Refuelling cost him the lead, but Ago, always the greatest of tacticians, played it cool and left his refuelling until he had sufficient time in hand over Roberts to be able to take the risk of a slow pit stop.

Watch out for this French rider, Michael Rougerie, whose ability on the tarmac is beginning to be felt. Rather an extrovert, his brief relationship with the big Harley has given him an impressive debut on the smaller H-D two strokes. Shown here riding a 750 Yamaha to second place at Imola, ten days after winning at Rouen, in 1976

Ago needn't have bothered too much. He rejoined the race, still in the lead and, despite a record lap by Roberts, finished 3.6s ahead, perhaps a little too close for comfort. Lansivouri came third and Gene Romero fourth, a brilliant European debut.

Imola '75 saw Cecotto win a race which few expected of him, although it would be fair to say that his performance at Daytona gave a reasonable indication that he would go well. He won both 100 mile legs, putting the decision beyond doubt in a race meeting which saw a determined Agostini break his own lap record over the twisty 3.136 mile circuit, eventually retiring when the coolant from his watercooled Yamaha escaped through a crack in the cylinder barrel. In spite of yet another tremendous ride, the bouncing Fin, Lansivouri, overdid it yet again when in a comfortably commanding lead and further enhanced the theory that Teppi was a rider who would either win, blow his machine up, or crash. Following closely upon the Match Races — previously Imola had come before the Easter series — neither Roberts nor Woods were very fit and Roberts eventually retired voluntarily with no feeling left in the hand he damaged at Oulton Park, Stan dropped the Suzuki GB machine for the second time in consecutive weekends. Back on board a Ducati after his lengthy layoff with a broken leg, Paul Smart also crashed and rebroke one of his legs, a similar accident to one which had kept him out of the saddle since the previous September's Race of the Year at Mallory Park. Rather like their domination of Daytona, Yamahas had an impressive seven machines leading the results.

The 200 had come to stay and Doctor Francesco Costa's efforts had not been in vain. Although Silverstone now boasts of two 100 mile races for the big bikes, it is not quite the same situation as that in Italy where the Motor Club Santerno have set the seal on a new and modern attitude in Europe. There is room for more meetings like the Imola 200, for while politicians debate whether or not to sanction a world championship series for 750cc machines, the world at large has given a very real answer to the wavering indecisions. There will probably be no better time for promoters and organisers to take advantage of the very obvious resurgance of interest in road racing for these big machines, but while others are slow to react in their hesitancy, Imola gets better and better.

6 Match race magic

Each Easter for the past six years, a series of races has been run over three of the most famous British circuits. For team riders from the United States of America and Great Britain, they have become affectionately known as the Match Races. The three circuits are Brands Hatch, situated south of London in Kent; Mallory Park in the heart of England's hunting country; and Oulton Park in Cheshire, probably the most picturesque of all three. These circuits change tempo slightly with the advent of Easter when the drab, black winter clouds should, in theory at least, give way to blue skies and spring daffodils. As any British inhabitant will tell you, only too frequently the vagaries of our climate are such as to preclude too much humour at this time of year. Even that greatest of all English authors, Shakespeare, has his words changed to "beware the ice in March"; perhaps a sentiment that should warn the Californian of what to expect. May be we are being too critical however, but it is a very evident truth that the weather, even at Easter, can be as contrary as an Irish hunter; at times producing total opposites on consecutive days.

This weather has played an all too important role in the fortunes of the visitors. In Britain and Europe races are started and finished in all but suicidal weather conditions, with the knowledge that the event cannot be either postponed or cancelled without serious difficulty. Racing schedules are so tight within the European community that the opportunity never exists for a re-run and, as a result, each sporting promotion is carefully balanced to take full advantage of, hopefully, good weather conditions. The British rider is therefore far better acclimatised than his American counterpart. His machines are set up for wet weather riding and his tyres reflect a design that has been developed over many years of mixed fortunes. Slicks are banned, under all but dry conditions.

Match races are not a new idea except in their modern concept. Speedway traditionally promotes match races, but only within the last six years has the idea caught on in road racing, as a direct result of the trans-Atlantic series run on Motor Circuit Development circuits. The original International Cup Races mentioned in an earlier chapter were run in Europe for competing teams from England, France, Austria, Denmark and Germany. Certainly, only England could these days field a strong enough team to take the United States to task. In strict contrast, the summer of 1911 saw the first match *race* between England and the United States, where two men squared up to each other over three separate races on the Brooklands track, as much for their own personal reputation as any national prestige. British champion Charlie Collier took on his American counterpart Jake de Rosier, both of them riding what we would now call the big bike. Charlie had his familiar 985 JAP-engined Matchless and Jake the slightly bigger Springfield-built 994 Indian. History records that Jake won two out of the three races and thus the match, but in reality the series could have gone either way. Within the context of match racing, this one-off event was not a very good example, but it is certainly interesting to note that it took exactly sixty years before another was staged, perhaps a significant sign of the way both Europe and the United States developed entirely separate characters.

In total contrast, the 800 horse power released from no less than thirty howling cylinders on 9th April 1971 was the culmination of years of planning, planning and hope which almost fell flat on its face many times before the drop of the first flag. It is appropriate to record that without Motor Circuit Developments, whose promotion has carried the series through five successful years, there would have been no match races today. This general statement leaves out many people who have had a hand in the overall success of the venture, notably the BSA/Triumph group who provided both men and machines for the first year, and John

Player & Sons whose sponsorship of the event over the last four years has been essential. Enthusiasm was the byword to success, and it was obvious from the word go that the riders were just as enthusiastic as the promoters, so I think all involved should share in the overall success of the venture.

The match races were destined to provide a much sought after link across the Atlantic to the greater benefit of the sport as a whole. Although Gary Nixon and Yvon DuHamel rode at Mallory Park in September 1970, the first match race was to break new ground in motorcycling history. Both Nixon and DuHamel were the first of the all-star American greats to ride in this country, and although American riders had preceded them, they had mostly met with derision. In the case of Sonny Angel, who arrived with a Yamaha in 1960 with a vast reputation and a brilliant orange jacket, perhaps contempt as well, since his performance wouldn't have done credit to any of our own Club riders. Ed La Belle had ridden the 500 BMW and Manx Norton with reasonable ability in the TT of 1959, but, on the whole, none of the American riders had shown a great deal of promise. The August 1969 edition of *Cycle World* summed up the situation quite fairly. "None of them served their time in the fierce struggle of AMA competition. Indeed they seemed to flee to foreign shores to avoid confrontation with the hot shoe crowd."

In 1954, the AMA re-organised their national championships to encompass all five types of racing which we, in Europe, would loosely term as road racing, speedway and moto-cross. The Grand National Champion was to be the rider who competed successfully in all types of racing, his earnings being based upon the points system which would eventually elect him to Champion status. Since little particular emphasis was placed on road racing (there were only a few road races within the year's schedule) the championship contenders had little opportunity to become expert on road race circuits, a situation which constantly improved up to and including 1975 when more and more road races became included in the AMA calendar. This allowed for a certain amount of specialisation but not enough to provide the expertise found outside America. The 1976 calendar was unstable at the time of writing and it looked, at one point, as though the AMA road racing schedule was going to revert to four a year.

Dave Aldana (USA)

It was important with the proposed match races that the American team should be composed of predominantly pavement specialists, because any team who were not able to compete successfully against our own riders would stand no chance at all on British circuits. The British short circuit rider had become renowned throughout Europe and even the proven international stars from the Continent found that they had to adapt their style and techniques to be successful. The scratcher title was one that was not all that far out in describing the type of rider and the type of racing in Britain. Five, ten, fifteen lap races over tight, twisting circuits, never over three miles in length, produced a particular breed of rider in Britain, a rider who, unless he took pains to broaden his horizon and ride some of the faster European circuits, tended to become type-cast under that very title. The British team rider therefore held faultless advantage on paper, and it was up to us to ensure that we helped to select the United States team from as stern a material as possible.

The second problem was much more political. Until the FIM Congress at Cannes in the October of 1970, when the AMA eventually became an integral part of the world motorcycling movement, American licences were not recognised in Europe. Any negotiations and plans up to that point had to be purely speculative, and I would like to think that the advent of closer competition across the Atlantic might have had some influence on the issue. Because the American road racing scene had been insular to a great extent, the ability to discuss plans for the future did not exist and any interchange of information was non-existent. Since it was obviously of prime importance to avoid promoting the series at a time of year when the AMA championship calendar interfered, a closer contact was essential, and to this end a series of communications had been started in 1969 with the then Executive Director of AMA, Bill Berry. I cannot say that the reaction was particularly encouraging but this partly led to a meeting at Daytona in March 1970 between Chris Lowe, Director of Motor Circuit Developments, myself, and Bill Berry, which happily led to a firm understanding which promised well. On April 29th Bill Berry resigned without leaving any of our discussions on record. A great deal of sheer determination was needed to re-open the issue with his successor Russ March and eventually, on July 30th, the Executive Committee of the AMA met to discuss amongst themselves the plans and hopes we all had for the proposed Match Races which were, even at that

Jim Rice (USA)

Derby's John Cooper who didn't distinguish himself too well during the first Match Races

stage, little more than an ambition. Contact had previously been made with some of the riders whom we thought might make up the team and although initial reaction was encouraging, it was little more than that. Dick O'Brien, Harley-Davidson Director of Engineering; Paul Garnant, Competitions Manager of Suzuki; Pete Colman, Triumph BSA Executive — all were reasonably impressed, but I had the feeling that life went at a much slower pace than ours and the ability to grasp what was meant by a Match Race between United States and Great Britain was not quite there. It seemed to have little appeal in the United States, to gauge the situation from their immediate reactions, which, I suppose, wasn't surprising when one considered the lack of importance of road racing within the AMA in those days. The scene has revolved once again, in that 1976 sees only four major road racing events, an abysmal attitude to one of the world's greatest spectator sports; abysmal to us, but understandable if the crowds are not there to pay for it.

Gary Lloyd Nixon seen sporting the Union Jack which confused some into wondering just which side he was on!

Before the AMA met, Dick O'Brien reported that he could not support the United States' team with Harley-Davidson riders, following the November 1969 rule change which left Harley's with a crash development programme. In spite of this disappointment, which immediately excluded the legendary Cal Rayborn, matters progressed slowly until November 1970, when Russ March reported that the AMA had left entirely free the required Easter period for the Match Races. This followed a meeting I had with him on behalf of MCD during the FIM Congress in Cannes, when we agreed, in principle, the regulations and other details on which the series would be based. Co-operation from AMA has always been of vital significance in the planning of the event and their continued enthusiasm through their new Executive Director, Ed Youngblood, continues to advance the liaison between Britain and America to mutual advantage and benefit.

In December came the news that the American riders were not at all keen to lose their dollar-earning

Dick Mann (USA)

Few riders have ever captured the hearts of the British motorcycling public as much as the late Cal Rayborn. He will never be forgotten by those who watched his cool and immaculate style

ability during the fortnight that they would be away, and that they required a guaranteed income, over and above their expenses and prize money which was due to be based upon their points totals. On January 1st 1971 the Match Races were abandoned, but Chris Lowe, MCD Director and man most responsible for new attitudes to racing in Britain, didn't give up quite so easily, and in February Peter Deverall, Marketing Director of BSA/Triumph, came forward with plans which would put both teams on three-cylinder machines. It didn't take too long to work out the details and, although there were more snags to come, the scene was set for the first of the now traditional Easter events, thanks to a lot of people. The AMA, ACU and FIM approved the regulations which would sanction the races; clutch starts were also approved (FIM regulations still enforced the European push start system for all but sidecar races) and so, on Good Friday 1971, old hopes were realised with ten riders sitting astride thirty cylinders on the startline at Brands Hatch.

Eligibility was simple; to allow for the contingency that machine breakdowns might stretch the number of 'threes' available, capacity limitations were set between 648 and 750cc. In case of emergency this would allow the use of the 650 Bonneville which had been so successful up to the introduction of the Trident and Rocket threes. No other limitations were imposed thus totally avoiding the unworkable and top-heavy rules that were widely being directed for use at the time. In point of fact as all the machines were the same there was little problem in any case. In the event, it transpired that the 'threes' were reliable enough to last out the series; although some original plans to run three races at each leg were modified to two, at the request of Doug Hele, who felt that three races were probably over-doing it a bit!

Riding for the United States were BSA Triumph works' riders Gary Nixon who was to act as captain; Veteran Dick Mann, Dave Aldana, Don Castro, Jim Rice and Don Emde — one of the riders to be held back as reserve in case personal injury should mar the series. Evergreen British veteran Percy Tait led the British team, ably backed by John Cooper, Paul Smart, Ray Pickrell and Tony Jefferies. The Americans were all Californians with a mixed background of successes, but certainly Gary Nixon, with his basic knowledge of Mallory Park at least, was reckoned to be a real threat to the obvious superior might of a British Team. Gary had won the 1967 and 1968 AMA Championship for Triumph which led to the confusing Union Flag on his leathers rather than his own Stars and Stripes! Dick Mann, although reasonably at home on pavement, was certainly far better on dirt, with a 1963 Grand National Championship already under his belt. David Aldana, master of Ascot, had already won the Talledega 200 mile road race, setting up a new average speed record; but even with this title to his already superior reputation it was doubted whether he would make too big a dent in the series. Don Castro, at that time, was considered to have unlimited road racing talent — as had Don Emde who had just pulled off a third place at Daytona. Jim Rice was very much a dirt star, this type of racing having taken him to second place in the AMA Championships.

British team captain Percy Tait was the oldest rider, at 42, with more road racing experience behind him than most of the other team members put together. British 750cc Champion, he had been chasing the circuits of Europe since 1948 and although he liked to point out that the P.H. in those days was his father, there were few who believed him! John Cooper had just won the Race of the Year for the second time; Ray Pickrell had just piloted the BSA triple into third place in South Africa, following his vast experience on Dunstall machines; Paul Smart just finished ahead of Ray in chasing the elusive Agostini in South African sunshine and Tony Jefferies, always a strong rider, concluded the line-up. Gary Nixon had trouble with Tony at the previous Race of the Year at Mallory, which had led to a few heated interchanges, perhaps a forewarning of the two completely different styles of riding.

The United States' team riders had been offered the opportunity to familiarise themselves with the British circuits in advance of the match races, which was perhaps unfortunate for team Captain Nixon, who fell off at Brands Hatch on the Wednesday, adding a wrist to his many orthopaedic breakages. Jim Rice, Dave Aldana and Dick Mann also had a narrow shave at Oulton Park when the hire car Jim was driving turned over at Lodge Corner on a topographical survey run, and virtually wrote itself off. There was no personal injury, only a few, long, unimpressed British visages.

There wasn't one British spectator who didn't sympathise with the Californians on the day of the opening round at Brands Hatch. The weather was cold and miserable. Even Gene Romero, who had come over as reigning American champion, found the dreary island weather unimpressive, and he was in the fortunate position of being able to watch — the other Americans had to get out there and ride! In the first of the two races over the 1.24 mile circuit, the American team was beaten by a mere five points, an impressive start by the inexperienced team. There was no stopping the flying Ray Pickrell, who learnt to race at Brands, being a

Harley-Davidson race chief Dick O'Brien with the Milwaukee factory's fastest ever four-stroke racer, the alloy engined ohv XR 750, during 1973

self-confessed coffee-bar cowboy, but his mature pace at the drop of the flag put those days far behind him. Both Dick Mann and Don Castro were impressive at their debut, learning something new on every lap, much to the delight of the strictly unpartisan crowd, who were probably suffering as much from climatic discomfort as the riders taking part. Although John Cooper never did like Brands Hatch, his trailing position made the crowds wonder whether his riding was strictly honest, particularly in view of the fact that he was no newcomer to big bike racing, having won the 1966 Hutchinson 100 for BSA on that very circuit, albeit the lengthier version of it. John repeated his ponderous position in the second race when, again, Pickrell scorched away winning easily, equalling the lap record with his meteoric progress. Paul Smart repeated his second position, ahead of Don Castro who had finally got the better of Dick Mann's low-line BSA. All told, the Americans were impressed with the British scene and certainly the home riders were favourably inclined towards the quick learning capacity of their protaganists.

From Brands Hatch the circus moved to Mallory Park, near Leicester; to the tight 1.35 mile circuit which was traditionally the Mecca of English motorcycle sport. It presented the American team with a problem they hadn't met before as it included a first gear hairpin which came at the end of fast section through S-bends; and also a one hundred and eighty degree bend that, seemingly, never ended. The Master of Mallory, John Cooper, hit back hard in front of his home crowd, equalling Mike Hailwood's Honda six lap record set in 1967, but even this rapid progress from a poor start couldn't catch the incredible Pickrell who won the first race with only four fifths of a second to spare from Cooper. Dick Mann was a creditable fourth. Only seven riders finished a race in which both Paul Smart and Percy Tait fell off. Don Castro, riding Gene Romero's Triumph, Jim Rice, Dave Aldana and Don Emde never did manage to get to grips with the hairpin and eventually lost contact with the rest of the field. During an interval race, Tony Jefferies also fell off, the resultant damage to his machine leaving only nine starters for the second of the match races. In spite of his record breaking ride John Cooper had to give best to Paul Smart and Ray Pickrell.

Although not an accomplished road racer, even the dirt track star has to maintain the factory image. Mert Lawwill on the factory Harley

An evening drive to Oulton Park saw the teams on the longer Cheshire circuit for Monday's races, providing a new challenge, particularly in view of the rather limited practice. Nixon had previously clocked a 1m52s lap but since he was not fit enough to race, the Americans lacked his expertise. Oulton Park is difficult enough to learn at the best of times, so on this occasion few gave the Americans much chance of making an impression. Both Percy Tait and Tony Jefferies had given the works' mechanics quite a lot of midnight effort during the quiet hours, Percy's championship winning machine needing new big-ends and Tony's a complete rebuild. In spite of the efforts, Percy again hit the dust in practice adding a few more bruises to his tally the day before. Both races were Paul Smart benefits. Pickrell was second in the first but fell off in the second at Knickerbrook, wrecking his machine. Dick Mann astonished everyone by finishing second to Paul Smart in that second race, finishing the series as the highest scoring American rider.

The final race at Oulton Park put the British team supreme in the series, not surprisingly, as an American victory was not really on the cards. The forty-six points which separated the teams at the end was not important. What was important was the friendliness and good sportsmanship in which the series had been run and the closer link it had forged between both countries. All riders had enjoyed themselves in what was, to them, a novel competition; and, without being too condescending, I think the American riders had benefitted a great deal by the experience gained on unusual circuits.

Trippe, Cox and Associates handled the 1972 team which was headed by double Daytona winner and ex-AMA Champion Calvin Rayborn. Three of the fastest machines in the world were also included, the 750 three-cylinder watercooled Suzukis, producing a reported 110 bhp. These machines were to be ridden by the American Suzuki squad of English expatriate Ron Grant, Art Baumann, and ex-Vietnam pilot Jody Nicholas. Dick Mann returned on his BSA and Don Emde was scheduled to ride the Vincent Davey prepared Kuhn Norton, on which he was also due to appear at Imola. Britain's world champion, Phil Read, was to lead the John Player Nortons, backed most ably by Peter Williams and new signing, Tony Rutter. Ray Pickrell, John Cooper and Tony Jefferies returned to complete the British line-up.

Conjecture made interesting reading. Would the three Suzukis tip the balance of power towards the American team; or would the superior handling ability of the Nortons offset the possible advantage? And what of the great Cal Rayborn, who had not ridden outside the United States before? Don Emde had just won Daytona, and although he was the first to admit that his experience on British circuits was a great help to him, would he be able to transmit his confidence to his new mount? Pickrell had remained at peak form throughout 1971, winning the Production TT on the 741 Triumph and finishing second in the new National Formula 750 Race to Tony Jefferies, whose knowledge and ability in the Isle of Man equated his somewhat meagre short circuit performances.

But the man who was to make 1972 his year was, without a doubt, the Californian from Woodside — Cal Rayborn — about whom John Cooper was to remark " ... this guy is bad news." Often claimed by the experts as the world's greatest road racer, Rayborn was often compared to Geoff Duke as both styles were similar; in fact Geoff had shown Cal round the TT circuit during an earlier, non-riding visit. All but one of Cal's National wins had been on road race circuits, the exception being the Livonia, Michigan Mile in 1971. He also held claim to the world's fastest motorcyclist, following his October 1970 successful crack at the world land speed record at the Bonneville Salt Flats where he piloted Harley-Davidson's single engine stream-liner at an average of 265.492mph. This record remains to this day in spite of Don Vesco's attempt which was not ratified by the FIM. Cal's machine was to be a privately-built Harley-Davidson, using one of his cast iron dirt engines and assembled by his ex-works' mechanic, Walt Falk. On this machine Cal stole three of the six races and finished second in the other three, sharing honours with Pickrell. The glory, however, went to Rayborn; his success staggered both British riders and spectators alike, who witnessed, for the first time, a rider of such supreme ability that, even with negligible practice, could take on the best of Britain's scratchers and win. His total practice at Brands Hatch and Mallory Park was of just a few laps' duration to evaluate his gearing and to familiarise himself with the circuit. At Mallory Park he knocked off one second a lap until he reached 53s and then packed it in, changing back into jeans and jacket. He didn't bother to take advantage of the Oulton Park practice, very alarming to those of us who were around to watch his performance on race day.

In the first Brands Hatch race Cal finished second to Ray Pickrell, ahead of world champion Phil Read and Norton's chief rider extraordinary, Peter Williams. Cal had shot into an early lead only to be overtaken by a very determined Pickrell, to whom the circuit was as familiar as his printing press. At the end of the race Pickrell shared a new lap record with Peter Williams at 81.75mph, the first time that the 80mph barrier had been broken; the previous record was shared by Ray, himself, and third place man Phil Read on a 350 Yamaha. Another surprise was the overgeared and oversteering Suzukis, which had nothing to offer except as a spectacle, there being plenty of scares on every lap to keep the spectators on their toes! The sheer power was unusable, perhaps because of the overgearing, but it was evident that the frame was quite incapable of taking the power pushed out by the monstrous motors, making their nickname of Flexy Fliers most apt for the occasion.

The second race saw Rayborn equal the new lap record with a run-away win from his shadow on the BSA. Again the two Andover 746 twin-cylinder Nortons were close behind, with Peter Williams, this time, getting the better of Phil Read. Peter had a real good go at Pick but the howl of the triple under acceleration was witness to the superior power which took it away from him every time.

During the Saturday rest day the Suzukis were fitted up with smaller engine sprockets which Suzuki GB team manager Rex White had fabricated at the McLaren factory in Surrey. But if Brands was to have proved unsuitable for the power-packed fliers, Mallory was to present a harder problem. The rapid right and left handed Esses proved to be a frame-twister if ever there was one: the Suzukis had little chance.

Rayborn, by this time, was on fine form and led Pickrell at the drop of the flag. Ray was having none of it and pegged him to second place around the long right-handed Gerards bend, and promptly pulled away to a clear win. John Cooper took third place, holding off the Norton challenge of Phil Read by the odd second. Trailing the field were the Suzukis and the lone Kuhn Norton of Don Emde, who had to take out a spare machine after his main mount had failed to start.

The second race was nothing short of outstanding, with Rayborn pulling away to a clear win over his, by now, arch rival Pickrell. Surprisingly, Jody Nicholas led the field in the opening stages but fought a losing battle with his untamed machine, which threatened to throw him into the nearest chasm, as it did at Brands Hatch during unofficial practice. Rayborn, once past, increased his lead, equalling Pickrell's fastest lap during the previous race and he eventually crossed the line six seconds ahead. John Cooper was again third but Jody Nicholas had kept the train on the track long enough to take a well deserved fourth place. The United States' team actually won this race on points.

Talking to Cal when he had first arrived in the U.K., he had remarked that his machine was a very much home-brewed effort as Dick O'Brien wasn't happy with his racing in England in case he got blown off. Walt Falk had prepared his dirt track engine as he had his works machine, and had stuck it in a modified frame especially for the match races. It was flown over from Miami with a small box of spares which was to see him through the series, and, even though the box contained almost a spare engine, Cal wanted to preserve the better tuned model as best he could. He spent little time practising, a puzzle which was answered at Oulton Park when he casually claimed that the engine would last only two hundred miles before going completely off song. His racing visit was gauged to the n'th degree! In the second race at Mallory, Rayborn had thrashed Pickrell and so shared two first and two seconds out of the four races to date. Two riders could not have been better matched. They arrived at Oulton Park in the knowledge that this was to be the tie breaker but there was little doubt that Pickrell would have the edge even though "Pick" didn't go at all well on the northern circuit. Cal's practice period had been very brief but, in spite of this, he went out in the first race and lost his constant shadow which left the supremacy result to the last race. The Suzukis proved more at home on the larger Oulton Park circuit but they managed no more than fifth, seventh and ninth places.

Rayborn led for nine laps of the second race until his machine went off song allowing Pickrell to coast home an easy winner. Jody Nicholas, more at home than his companions, went far better and trailed John Cooper into fourth place. Britain again won the series for the second time but Rayborn and Pickrell ended even at the conclusion of the match races and shared the fastest laps on all circuits between them, including a new lap record at Brands Hatch. The total points scored were USA 211; GB 255, exactly the same difference as 1971. The vee-twin Harley-Davidson had proved to be quite an eye-opener! Rayborn claimed that Pickrell was "the greatest rider I have ever raced against", a sentiment that was readily echoed by Ray, who had been shattered by his rapid progress and easy learning ability. The Harley's handling was as impeccable as its rider, which was more than could be said of the Suzuki threesome, riding machines based upon the GT750 which had first put in an appearance at the Tokyo Motorcycle Show the previous November. Their speed wasn't in question, but that's where their advantage ended.

By 1973, the match races at Easter were an eagerly anticipated part of the British racing season, but team problems had changed the format, particularly following the BSA/Triumph withdrawal from racing which had partly led to Ray Pickrell's retirement. Ray had also crashed very heavily in the 1972 September Race of the Year at Mallory Park and felt that his career had come to an end. The rest of 1972 had been crowned in glory following the match races, during which the flying Pickrell was seldom headed. He won both Production races in the Isle of Man — one of them for Formula 750 machines — and set a record lap of 105.68mph on his fourth lap of the 37¾ mile mountain circuit. His record race average was 104.23mph for the one-hour and forty-eight minute race!

It was safely predicted that the Americans could win for the first time, but the continuity of past team members with experience of British circuits was lacking. Furthermore, the weather which was the deciding factor for the most part, had yet to put in its worst performance. On circuits which were used each and every weekend, wet weather generally required an entirely different approach, particularly if rain fell on an already greasy surface, mainly rubber left from previous dry meetings.

Newcomers to the United States' team were Mert Lawwill, ex-AMA champion of 1969, who replaced the injured Mark Brelsford whose Daytona crash was as spectacular as it was final to the ambitions of this brilliant rider, Doug Sehl, Dave's brother, who joined Mert in the work's Harley-Davidson team, and the full Bob Hansen works' Kawasaki team of Garry Nixon, Yvon DuHamel and Art Baumann. Ron Grant was mounted on the lone American-entered Suzuki and Dave Aldana on a British-supplied Norton. All eyes were on Rayborn, who brought the new XR750 Harley-Davidson, but no one expected too much of him due to his crash at Daytona, which broke his shoulder. Cal had returned for the Race of the Year but magneto trouble stopped him in his quest to take on the Finnish star Jarno Saarinen. Having returned to the States his experience in England stood him in good stead during the rest of 1972. He won at Laguna Seca, came third at Indianapolis and put up the fastest time at Ontario before his challenge faded out during the race proper. These results ended three years of comparative drought for Cal, broken only by his superb English performances.

Dave Potter brought off a surprise win at Brands Hatch in 1975 on Ted Broad's Yamaha

Into the United States team for the first time came Pat Hennen

Don Castro tried to take the inside line on Britain's Pat Mahoney at the Mallory Park hairpin. He failed on this occasion

Stan Woods didn't have much luck at Mallory Park in 1975, falling off in the first race and damaging his hand. This is a practice shot taken as he pushes Bob Heath wide

Brothers-in-Law Barry Sheene and Paul Smart led the British team with 750cc Suzukis. Paul had won at Ontario by an aggregate of one fifth of a second and had finished fourth at Talledega behind DuHamel, Nixon and Baumann. Barry had become 750cc Champion, having turned down a lucrative Yamaha contract, and Mick Grant was mounted on a Boyer Triumph in place of the Seeley Kawasaki, which did not come to fruition. John Cooper had changed camps to Norton alongside Peter Williams, and Dave Potter, British 750cc Champion, had out his familiar Kuhn Norton. Tony Jefferies was again mounted on a very private Triumph three.

Both British-entered Suzukis were expected to perform better than last year's American models and the latest monocoque Nortons had obvious handling advantages, even if they did lack that ultimate speed. The Harleys had a superb reputation but both Lawwill and Sehl lacked the experience necessary on British short circuits.

The treacherously greasy surface in the first race at Brands brought down a number of riders, not the least of whom were Ron Grant, Paul Smart, Cal Rayborn and Peter Williams. The race was eventually won by Dave Potter, Tony Jefferies also having missed the first two races when he crashed in practice, his place being taken by another ex-British Champion, Ron Chandler. He too had joined the list of fallen in the first race. At the conclusion of the first two Brands rounds, the Americans were in the lead, and the impeccable Cal Rayborn was, once again, stamping his authority on the series, winning the second race from Paul Smart and, at the same time, equalling the 1972 record on the 335lb, four-speed machine. John Cooper had fallen off his 350 Yamsel in an earlier race and was in no fit state to continue, Dave Croxford stepping into the breach.

Rain at Mallory led to a reduction in laps, from the twenty-two planned to the fifteen actually run. Fortunes were inconsistent, Peter Williams taking twelve laps to get through the Kawasaki's defence of Nixon, DuHamel and Baumann. Barry Sheene had trouble with a tyre just before he was to wheel out onto the start line, and changed to his 500 grand prix machine, only to fall off and later be excluded from the results as a consequence of his strictly illegal substitution. Doug Sehl, who had only ridden in five road races before his inclusion in the United States' team, had been replaced by Gary Fisher. Sehl fell twice at Brands Hatch in the second match race and fractured a collar bone. DuHamel gave his finest performance ever at Mallory and scored first and third places to take overall points lead at the conclusion of the four races. Jefferies was back in the team after frantic repairs to his machine, but Mick Grant crashed his Boyer Triumph, putting it completely out of action.

Teams went to Oulton Park with thirteen points separating them. The rain which had threatened to destroy the series stopped just in time for the first race, which was run on a wet circuit. The visitors won the first race by five points which decreased their deficit. A superb race by Peter Williams put the first place outside any doubt and a repeat performance in the second race left the series in Britain's pocket, only two points separating the two teams at the end. The British press had predicted widely differing points margins, but it had always been part of the regulations for the match races that only finishers would count towards the final points positions, and although riders who had fallen by the wayside during the race would be personally credited with points on which to calculate their cash awards, these would have to be left out of the final reckoning. Such casualties in the first race had been Dave Potter, who suffered from a seized gearbox, Tony Jefferies, whose slightly overworked machine broke down, and Barry Sheene, with a loose filler cap on his radiator causing overheating problems. Paul Smart came a cropper in the second race on a drying track, and on only the second lap. The other casualty was Doug Sehl's Harley-Davidson — blown up in a big way by Gary Fisher — which brought Englishman Cliff Carr into the team to make up for the depleted numbers starting the second race. Mick Grant had switched to John Cooper's Daytona Norton, following his Mallory Park debacle, on which he put in a final sprint to elevate the British team total. None of those present for that final race knew quite how close the United States had got to winning their first match race! Only in the final analysis, when the dust had settled, could one sit down quietly and work out the points. America had almost pulled it off — but not quite!

After the competition, AMA Director of Competition Don Woods was quoted as saying that the Match Races had been a raw deal for the Americans as they had intended that Paul Smart should represent United States. Paul had already represented Britain in the first match races in 1971 so it was difficult to concede the validity of the point he was making. Although Paul, rather like Cliff Carr, was spending much of his time racing in the United States — hence the reason why Cliff was brought in at the very last minute to equate the teams — there was no way in which he could be counted as an American! It could have been added that Cliff Carr's eight points had almost drawn the series!

By the time 1974 had dawned upon the horizon, both Daytona and Imola had been run, and won by Giacomo Agostini on his new mount, the 703 TZ700 Yamaha to which camp he had changed at the conclusion of the previous year. A twenty-two year old American from Modesto, California had come second on both occasions: his name — Kenny Roberts. Virtually unknown before 1973, he had risen quickly from novice ranks had joined Yamaha and, under the superb guidance of the wily Australian Kel Carruthers, had won the coveted number one title for the first time. His impact upon the 1974 match races was to be as staggering as that of Cal Rayborn, who had met an untimely death in New Zealand riding a Suzuki in January. A faster combination had seldom been witnessed in England, and whereas it was too much to expect him to win everything, he had a pretty good stab at it during the short spell he was here.

On Friday, 12th April the short-haired, diminutive Roberts, looking for all the world as though he had just left high-school — actually he never even completed more than his junior year — rocketed to second place at Brands Hatch, setting a new lap record in the process. Only Paul Smart managed to salvage some British pride with a hard-pressed win, when Kenny was showered with hot water by his Yamaha, momentarily dropping him to third place. Yvon DuHamel had led for eight laps on the mighty Kawasaki until it seized, and only then were the British riders able to take advantage of the respite to pull themselves together. Art Baumann also had to retire with a misfiring Kawasaki, which allowed British team riders to take advantage, once again, of midfield places and to gain important points. Reserve American rider Jim Evans was brought into the team when John Long discovered a nail in his tyre — the second pucnture he had suffered in as many days — and managed a tenth place on his very much non-works TZ700. The British team led by twenty points at the end of this opening round, which would have been more but for the fact that Mick Grant added to his match race reputation by crashing yet again. Both Peter Williams and Percy Tait suffered mechanical failures, it being reported that Peter had lost a gear lever and Percy had seized his Triumph triple engine. Roberts dropped the lap record to 54s, advancing himself beyond even his fellow countryman Rayborn, who had set the pace the year before with 54.6s. British Suzukis in the hands of Barry Sheene and Stan Woods had been quick to settle third and fourth places, which meant that works Suzukis had taken three out of the first four places.

At the start of the second race Roberts was quickly into the lead but on the fifth lap "Superfrog" DuHamel forced his way in front on his now repaired air-cooled Kawasaki and was never headed, equalling the new lap record, a time again shared in this race with a consistent Roberts. Paul Smart had to be content with third place, and with Gary Nixon taking fifth place from Stan Woods behind the other Suzuki of Sheene, points were shared at sixty-eight apiece. The United States trailed to Mallory Park twenty points in arrears.

The Brands Hatch wet weather, which had proved a thorough dampener, gave way to a bright day at Mallory, with sun spilling down from the skies onto a record crowd. Kenny Roberts won both races and set up yet another lap record when he equalled Jarno Saarinen and Phil Read's 50.6s. Gary Nixon improved his placings with third and fourth positions, while Romero, too, pulled himself together to join team-mate Gary in the battle for points. Yvon had come off in practice — twice — once at Gerards and once at the Esses, suffering from the engine problems which had affected his opening gambit at Brands Hatch. Barry Sheene had put in two lightning performances, leading the opening half of the first race until being baulked by John Long, who let Roberts through like a flash. In the second, he again took half the race to oust Gary Nixon from second position; the two Suzukis rounded the Hairpin side by side,wheels pawing the air in the battle for supremacy, an impressive sight for those privileged to watch. DuHamel's Kawasaki let him down yet again while running in fourth place and Paul Smart crashed heavily at the Esses. Percy Tait's Triumph seized again, which put the United States thirty-nine points adrift as they went to Oulton Park for the final two rounds.

It wasn't a happy team of American riders who travelled the sixty odd miles to Cheshire that Sunday evening. The prospect of two ten lap races over a circuit that had so far proved encouraging was hopeful in itself, but the deficit was such that it would take a lot of hard riding and a certain amount of luck to pull back. There was no mistaking the determination for, although Barry Sheene was unbeatable in the opening round with such a searing pace that he broke the lap record, Roberts, Nixon, Romero and Aldana filled four of the first six places. The Americans pulled back thirteen points giving them a possible victory if only they could gain midfield points as well. Roberts went out in the second race and won his third race of the series. Second was Sheene, and this time Romero was up to third place. But bad luck hit the United States' team

Surprise success for Pat Mahoney who finished second in the first of the 1975 Match Races

Standing to attention was just one of the practice poses that Steve Baker enjoyed, though I bet his hands were hot!

Dave Aldane, as always, at home wherever he went, enjoys a crack by Romero

Steve McLoughlin found his baptism in England a little harder than anticipated, but showed good progress and a great degree of humour

Charlie Williams joined the British squad as a reserve rider, succeeding, in fact, to take his place on the start line

Showing no mercy to British hearts, team captain Kenny Roberts steams out of the hairpin at Mallory to record yet another win and fastest lap

Pat Hennen emulates his captain but has trouble getting both wheels in line

two laps from the end when Gary Nixon, well in the hunt up to that point, retired from a lack of fuel. Too little had been put in his tank at the start and with the petrol, drained too the chances of an American victory. The final race had been won by the United States by seven points. The overall difference at the end of the series was nineteen points; twenty points had been pulled back during the last two races.

It would be difficult to summarise the races up to, and including, 1974. There could seldom have been a more interesting and more closely fought series of races in the history of motorcycling, but it could be said that the British circuits favoured the better prepared machines run by the British team. Although they had their moments of success, the H2R Kawasakis never proved themselves very reliable, which probably meant the difference between success and failure. This could also have applied to the American Suzukis which were certainly not the best of handlers. The John Player Nortons were well suited to their home territory but the most surprising machine of all was Cal Rayborn's hastily-prepared Harley-Davidson. The TZ700 Yamaha, banned by the FIM at the beginning of 1974 because of homologation rules, was by far the best of all the Superbikes, being more suitably prepared for the British circuits with a surprising inbuilt reliability that must have staggered even the manufacturers! British circuits are not the easiest to learn and it is with all due credit to each American visitor that he had competed safely and successfully in England, on circuits the like of which he rarely saw anywhere in his own country.

The tide turned in 1975 for although the home side still had a good team, the United States' team showed real force for the very first time; force in as much as the machinery was certainly impressive and the team was strong throughout, albeit with a number of new faces. The cards were stacked in favour of the Americans, not so much because of this paper strength, but nobody really believed that Britain could win this time out. As it happened they didn't, a fact which was welcomed as much at home as in America. Why Britain didn't win is a matter for conjecture but there was no wondering what the visitors had going for them that Britain didn't — sheer determination to succeed, that gritty compound which was shared by every member of the party from team captain Kenny Roberts down to the new faces of Pat Hennen, Phil McDonald

Even three years ago it would have been unheard of for an American to gain laurels at a British meeting. 1975 saw Roberts at the peak of his determination to prove that he is undoubtedly amongst the top three in the world

Steve McLaughlin and Steve Baker. Their machinery included the three works TZ750s which were to be ridden by Roberts, Romero and Castro; the TZ700s of Baker, McLaughlin, McDonald and reserve rider Randy Cleek; and the works Suzukis of Aldana and Hennen, the latter having had quite a fantastic start to his racing season by winning the Marlborough series in New Zealand, just ahead of his fellow American Randy Cleek.

It was almost certain that Roberts would dominate the series as he had the previous year and equally obvious that both Romero and Castro would provide an adequate back-up throughout. Romero had just won at Daytona and it was becoming increasingly apparent that here was a rider who would not relinquish his reputation as easily as some. The Suzuki-mounted Aldana had yet to show his mettle, mainly due to the fact that he had fallen during the Kawasaki Superbike International and fractured his pelvis. His appearance on the Suzuki at Daytona had been unimpressive but he did win the supporting production race on a 900 Kawasaki. With McLaughlin in the team as well, it was an imposing team that turned out for the first race meeting at Brands Hatch — only to have the weather cancel the meeting!

I have never been able to understand why the Easter holiday period has not been fixed to take advantage of the improving weather conditions of a late British Spring. I seem to remember being told at school that Easter Sunday was on the first Sunday after the first full moon after the Vernal Equinox (or something like that anyway) which means that there can be a difference of almost a month from year to year. This particular year Easter Sunday was to fall on March 30th so the Match Races were to be held on the 28th, 30th and 31st; far too early for even the hardiest of temperaments. We all shivered as the snow destroyed the first of the Match Races, and even though the sun got up after a long morning in bed, its strength was not enough to clear the circuit and verges so that racing could take place. There was no hope of clearing the circuit by artificial means whether by salting or bulldozing to assist Mother Nature. Either attempt would have only added to the problems which were obviously destined to cancel the first two races of the 1975 series.

One of the fastest men in Britain in 1975 was Mick Grant, but he decided to give the weather conditions best during the opening round

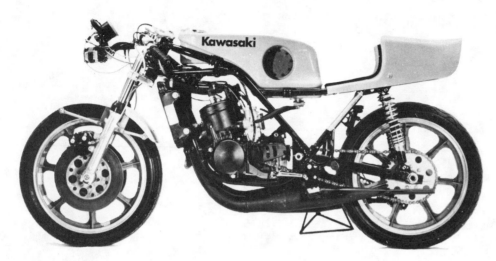

1975 HR750 Kawasaki. Water cooled three cylinder. The fuel tank takes 5.28 gallons

By total contrast, Mallory Park, only 140 miles away, was as clear as a bell. The crisp cold air kept the snow away during Friday and Saturday but by Sunday it looked as though the threatening sky would justify those pessimists who reckoned that the whole of the series was doomed. The first of the two races was started in sunshine and ended in a flurry of snow which made the latter stages of the race so hazardous that Mick Grant gave it best and retired. Every rider taking part was mounted on slick tyres and as the race progressed the amount of adhesion deteriorated. But in spite of the obvious discomfort, the American captain, Kenny Roberts, finished his race a resounding first, giving the appearance of an almost untroubled ride, which would have done him credit in the warmth of California. Wearing the normal British wet weather oversuit, he took the lead on the third lap and carefully increased it until the flag dropped. Britain's Pat Mahoney, on yet another TZ700 Yamaha, took a superb second place, ahead of the rapidly improving Aldana. At the end of the first lap Britain's 750 Champion Stan Woods had fallen off at Devil's Elbow, attempting to keep with Roberts, and the Canadian Steve Baker had a similar experience at the Esses, right in front of Dave Potter, who was riding the Ted Broad Yamaha. Another faller at the Esses was Gene Romero but conscious of his team's points he remounted a rather bent machine to finish the race.

The weather worsened, the snow shower changed to rain and everyone switched to wet weather tyres, the Americans opting for hand-cut GoodYears. The race distance for the second race was changed from the twenty planned laps to just fifteen, due to the worsening conditions, and with Randy Cleek replacing the injured Baker and Charlie Williams in place of Stan Woods, the riders looked forward apprehensively to the start of the second and last of the Mallory Park matches. After the first race defeat at the hands of the Americans, who had shot into a sixteen point lead, worse was to come for the already demoralised Britains. At the end of the first lap Roberts led Aldana and Romero. Dave Croxford managed to take the outpaced Norton up into fourth place but fell foul of the Esses, remounting to ride on with his gearbox jammed in third. Don Castro picked off the two Kawasakis of Mick Grant and Barry Ditchburn and it was a sorry picture which emerged when the flag dropped after the second race. It almost went without saying that Roberts won the second race as well, but Aldana finished second and Don Castro third, so the points were all in favour of the Americans as machines and wet clothing were packed off to Oulton Park for the following day's meeting.

A shortened 1.654 mile circuit was introduced at Oulton Park for the first time in 1975 so both the teams were very much equated for this event. Roberts, Romero and Aldana romped away with the first race, to add to their already impressive points total, under equally arduous weather conditions. But it was a close thing in the second race when Roberts and Romero both fell. This let a marginally recovered Stan Woods into first place on his home circuit and a determined Pat Mahoney into second, and while Pat Hennen finished third and Don Castro fourth, it allowed the British team to record their first race win of the series, finishing some six points ahead of the Americans. The effort came too late in the day and while Roberts and Romero seethed by the trackside at letting the side down, there was no way that Britain could have pulled it off other than by a landslide. In spite of the rain and the cold Kenny Roberts and his team were delighted that they had pulled off the first win in five years, and well they should have been!

Anglo-American Match Race Results *1971*

9th April — Brands Hatch
Circuit length 1.24 miles
2 races each of 12 laps

Race 1			Race 2		
1st	R. Pickrell	(BSA) — in 12m.11s at 73.28mph	1st	R. Pickrell — in 11m.28.6s at 77.79mph	
2nd	P. A. Smart	(Triumph)	2nd	P. A. Smart	
3rd	D. Mann	(BSA)	3rd	D. Castro	
4th	P. H. Tait	(Triumph)	4th	D. Mann	
5th	D. Emde	(BSA)	5th	P. H. Tait	
6th	D. Castro	(Triumph)	6th	A. M. Jefferies	
7th	D. Aldana	(BSA)	7th	D. Emde	
8th	A. M. Jefferies	(Triumph)	8th	D. Aldana	
9th	J. Rice	(BSA)	9th	J. Rice	
10th	J. H. Cooper	(BSA)	10th	J. H. Cooper	

Fastest Lap: Mann in 58.2s at 76.70mph
Points: USA — 25. GB — 30.

Fastest Lap: Pickrell in 56.2s at 79.43mph
(Equals record)
Points: USA — 24. GB — 31.

14th April — Mallory Park
Circuit length 1.35 miles
2 races each of 11 laps

Race 1		Race 2	
1st	R. Pickrell — 10m.8.8s at 88.54mph	1st	P. A. Smart — 9m.55.8s at 89.72mph
2nd	J. H. Cooper	2nd	R. Pickrell
3rd	D. Mann	3rd	J. H. Cooper
4th	A. M. Jefferies	4th	D. Mann
5th	D. Emde	5th	D. Castro
6th	D. Aldana	6th	D. Aldana
7th	J. Rice	7th	J. Rice
		8th	D. Emde

Fastest Lap: Smart & Pickrell in 53.6s at 90.67mph
Points: USA — 23. GB — 26.

Fastest Lap: Cooper in 52s at 93.46mph
(Equals record)
Points: USA — 25. GB — 27.

15th April — Oulton Park
Circuit length 2.75 miles
2 races each of 5 laps

Race 1		Race 2	
1st	P. A. Smart — 9m.05.6s at 91.09mph	1st	P. A. Smart — 9m.09.6s at 90.43mph
2nd	R. Pickrell	2nd	D. Mann
3rd	J. H. Cooper	3rd	J. H. Cooper
4th	D. Mann	4th	P. H. Tait
5th	P. H. Tait	5th	A. M. Jefferies
6th	A. M. Jefferies	6th	J. Rice
7th	D. Emde	7th	D. Castro
8th	J. Rice	8th	D. Aldana
9th	D. Aldana	9th	D. Emde
10th	D. Castro		

Fastest Lap: Smart in 1m.47.2s at 92.72mph
Points: USA — 17. GB — 38.

Fastest Lap: Smart in 1m.48.2s at 91.86mph
Points: USA — 23. GB — 31.
Final Totals: Unites States — 137 points
              Great Britain — 183 points

1971 — **How they scored**

	Round 1	Round 2	Round 3	Round 4	Round 5	Round 6	Total
GREAT BRITAIN							
R. Pickerell	10	10	10	9	9		48
P. A. Smart	9	9		10	10	10	48
P. H. Tait	7	6			6	7	26
A. M. Jefferies	3	5	7		5	6	26
J. H. Cooper	1	1	9	8	8	8	35
	30	31	26	27	38	31	183
UNITED STATES							
D. Mann	8	7	8	7	7	9	46
D. Castro	5	8		6	1	4	24
D. Aldana	4	3	5	5	2	3	22
J. Rice	2	2	4	4	3	5	20
D. Emde	6	4	6	3	4	2	25
	25	24	23	25	17	23	137

John Player TransAtlantic Trophy Results   *1972*

31st March — Brands Hatch
2 races each of 20 laps

Race 1
1st	R. Pickrell	(Triumph) — 18m.36.8s at 80.94mph
2nd	C. Rayborn	(Harley-Davidson)
3rd	P. W. Read	(Norton)
4th	P. Williams	(Norton)
5th	D. Mann	(BSA)
6th	D. Emde	(Kuhn Norton)
7th	J. H. Cooper	(BSA)
8th	A. Baumann	(Suzuki)
9th	J. Nicholas	(Suzuki)
10th	A. M. Jefferies	(Triumph)
11th	T. Rutter	(Norton)

Fastest Lap: (Record) Pickrell & Williams in 54.6s at 81.75mph
Points: USA — 35. GB — 42.

Race 2
1st	C. Rayborn — 18m.36.4s at 80.97mph	
2nd	R. Pickrell	
3rd	P. Williams	
4th	P. W. Read	
5th	J. H. Cooper	
6th	A. Baumann	
7th	R. Grant	(Suzuki)
8th	J. Nicholas	
9th	D. Mann	
10th	A. M. Jefferies	
11th	T. Rutter	

Fastest Lap: Rayborn in 54.6s at 81.75mph
(Equals new record)
Points: USA —34. GB — 43.

2nd April — Mallory Park
Two races each of 18 laps

Race 1
1st	R. Pickrell — 16m.7s at 90.46mph
2nd	C. Rayborn
3rd	J. H. Cooper
4th	P. W. Read
5th	D. Mann
6th	A. M. Jefferies
7th	A. Baumann
8th	R. Grant
9th	P. Williams
10th	J. Nicholas
1ith	D. Emde

Fastest Lap: Pickrell in 52.8s at 92.05mph
Points: USA — 35. GB — 42.

Race 2
1st	C. Rayborn — 16m.12.8s at 89.92mph
2nd	R. Pickrell
3rd	J. H. Cooper
4th	J. Nicholas
5th	P. W. Read
6th	A. Baumann
7th	P. Williams
8th	D. Mann
9th	R. Grant
10th	D. Emde
11th	T. Rutter
12th	A. M. Jefferies

Fastest Lap: Rayborn in 52.8s at 92.05mph
Points: USA — 40. GB — 38.

3rd April — Oulton Park
Two races each of 9 laps

Race 1
1st	C. Rayborn — 16m. 16.2s at 91.64mph
2nd	R. Pickrell
3rd	J. H. Cooper
4th	P. Williams
5th	J. Nicholas
6th	P. W. Read
7th	R. Grant
8th	A. M. Jefferies
9th	A. Baumann
10th	D. Mann
11th	T. Rutter
12th	D. Emde

Fastest Lap: Rayborn in 1m.46.4s at 93.42mph
Points: USA — 34. GB — 44.

Race 2
1st	R. Pickrell — 16m.06.6s at 92.55mph
2nd	C. Rayborn
3rd	J. H. Cooper
4th	J. Nicholas
5th	P. Williams
6th	P. W. Read
7th	A. M.Jefferies
8th	R. Grant
9th	D. Mann
10th	D. Emde

Fastest Lap: Pickrell & Rayborn in 1m.46.0s at 93.77mph
Points: USA — 32. GB — 43.
Final Totals: United States — 210 points
Great Britain — 252 points

1972 — How they scored

	Round 1	Round 2	Round 3	Round 4	Round 5	Round 6	Total
GREAT BRITAIN							
R. Pickrell	12	11	12	11	11	12	69
P. W. Read	10	9	9	8	7	7	50
P. Williams	9	10	4	6	9	8	46
J. H. Cooper	6	8	10	10	10	10	54
A. M. Jefferies	3	3	7	1	5	6	25
T. Rutter	2	2		2	2		8
	42	43	42	38	44	43	252
UNITED STATES							
C. Rayborn	11	12	11	12	12	11	69
D. Mann	8	4	8	5	3	4	32
D. Emde	7		2	3	1	3	16
A. Baumann	5	7	6	7	4		29
J. Nicholas	4	5	3	9	8	9	38
R. Grant		6	5	4	6	5	26
	35	34	35	40	34	32	210

John Player TransAtlantic Trophy Results   *1973*

20th April — Brands Hatch
Two races each of 24 laps

Race 1
1st	D. Potter	(Kuhn Norton) — 22m.52.8s	
		at 78.04mph	
2nd	Y. DuHamel	(Kawasaki)	
3rd	D. Sehl	(Harley-Davidson)	
4th	A. Baumann	(Kawasaki)	
5th	G. Nixon	(Kawasaki)	
6th	D. Aldana	(John Player Norton)	
7th	J. Cooper	(John Player Norton)	
8th	M. Lawwill	(Harley-Davidson)	
9th	P. H. Tait	(Triumph)	

Fastest Lap: Rayborn & Williams in 55.2s at 80.87mph
Points: USA — 74. GB — 34.

Race 2
1st	C. Rayborn — 22m.30.4s at 79.34mph		
2nd	P. A. Smart		
3rd	P. Williams		
4th	Y. DuHamel		
5th	D. Potter		
6th	B. Sheene		
7th	G. Nixon		
8th	A. Baumann		
9th	J. H. Cooper		
10th	R. Chandler	(Triumph)	
11th	M. Lawwill		
12th	M. Grant		
13th	D. Aldana		
14th	P. H. Tait		

Fastest Lap: Rayborn in 54.6s at 81.76mph
(Equals record)
Points: USA — 58. GB — 75.

22nd April — Mallory Park
Two races each of 15 laps
(Reduced by reason of bad weather)

Race 1
1st	P. Williams — 14m.46.4s at 82.84mph
2nd	G. Nixon
3rd	Y. DuHamel
4th	D. Croxford
5th	D. Potter
6th	A. Baumann
7th	M. Grant
8th	P. H. Tait
9th	P. A. Smart
10th	A. M. Jefferies
11th	M. Lawwill
12th	C. Rayborn
13th	G. Fisher (Harley-Davidson)
14th	R. Grant
15th	D. Aldana

Fastest Lap: Williams, Nixon & DuHamel in 56.0 at 86.78mph
Points: USA — 60. GB — 75.

Race 2
1st	Y. DuHamel — 13m.33s at 89.67mph
2nd	P. Williams
3rd	P. A. Smart
4th	C. Rayborn
5th	D. Potter
6th	P. H. Tait
7th	A. Baumann
8th	B. Sheene
9th	D. Aldana
10th	G. Fisher (Harley-Davidson)
11th	M. Lawwill
12th	G. Nixon
13th	R. Grant
14th	A. M. Jefferies

Fastest Lap: Smart & Williams in 52.8s at 92.05mph
Points: USA — 69. GB — 64.

23rd April — Oulton Park
Two races each of 11 laps

Race 1
1st	P. Williams — 21m.42.6s at 83.94mph
2nd	P. A. Smart
3rd	A. Baumann
4th	D. Croxford
5th	D. Aldana
6th	Y. DuHamel
7th	M. Grant
8th	C. Rayborn
9th	C. Carr
10th	P. H. Tait
11th	G. Nixon
12th	M. Lawwill
13th	R. Grant
14th	A. M. Jefferies

Fastest Lap: Smart in 1m.54.8s at 86.58mph
Points: USA — 69. GB — 64.

Race 2
1st	P. Williams — 20m.13.6s at 90.09mph
2nd	Y. DuHamel
3rd	B. Sheene
4th	P. H. Tait
5th	G. Nixon
6th	C. Rayborn
7th	D. Croxford
8th	M. Grant
9th	A. M. Jefferies
10th	M. Lawwill
11th	R. Grant
12th	D. Potter
13th	D. Aldana

Fastest Lap: Williams in 1m.48.2s at 91.86mph
Points: USA — 55. GB — 75.
Final Totals: United States — 385 points
Great Britain — 387 points

1973 — How they scored

	Round 1	Round 2	Round 3	Round 4	Round 5	Round 6	Total
GREAT BRITAIN							
D. Potter	16	12	12	12		5	57
P. A. Smart		15	8	14	15		52
J. H. Cooper	10	8					18
P. H. Tait	8	3	9	11	7	13	51
P. Williams		14	16	15	16	16	77
B. Sheene		11		9		14	34
M. Grant		5	10		10	9	34
R. Chandler							302
D. Croxford		7	13		13	10	43
A. M. Jefferies			7	3	3	8	21
	34	75	75	64	64	75	387
UNITED STATES							
Y. DuHamel	15	13	14	16	11	15	84
C. Rayborn		16	5	13	9	11	54
D. Sehl	14						14
M. Lawwill	9	6	6	6	5	7	39
A. Baumann	13	9	11	10	14		57
G. Nixon	12	10	15	5	6	12	60
D. Aldana	11	4	2	8	12	4	41
G. Fisher			4	7			11
C. Carr					8		8
R. Grant			3	4	4	6	17
	74	58	60	69	69	55	385

John Player TransAtlantic Trophy Results   *1974*

12th April — Brands Hatch
Two races each of 22 laps

Race 1
1st	P. A. Smart	(Suzuki) — 20m.22.2s at 80.35mph
2nd	K. Roberts	(Yamaha)
3rd	B. Sheene	(Suzuki)
4th	S. Woods	(Suzuki)
5th	B. Ditchburn	(Yamaha)
6th	D. L. Croxford	(JP Norton)
7th	D. Aldana	(JP Norton)
8th	G. Nixon	(Suzuki)
9th	E. Romero	(Yamaha)
10th	J. Evans	(Yamaha)
11th	G. Fisher	(Yamaha)
12th	P. Williams	(JP Norton)
13th	P. H. Tait	(Triumph)

Fastest Lap: Roberts in 54. at 82.67mph
(Record)
Points: USA — 55. GB — 75.

Race 2
1st	Y. DuHamel	(Kawasaki) — 20m.12.8s at 80.97mph
2nd	K. Roberts	
3rd	P. A. Smart	
4th	B. Sheene	
5th	G. Nixon	
6th	S. Woods	
7th	D. L. Croxford	
8th	B. Ditchburn	
9th	P. Williams	
10th	D. Aldana	
11th	E. Romero	
12th	A. Baumann	(Kawasaki)
13th	G. Fisher	
14th	J. Long	(Yamaha
15th	M. Grant	(Kawasaki)
16th	P. H. Tait	(Kuhn Norton)

Fastest Lap: Roberts and DuHamel at 54s at 82.67mph
(Equals new record)
Points: USA — 68. GB — 68.

14th April — Mallory Park
Two races each of 20 laps

Race 1
1st	K. Roberts — 17m.25.6s at 92.96mph
2nd	B. Sheene
3rd	P. A. Smart
4th	G. Nixon
5th	S. Woods
6th	E. Romero
7th	P. H. Tait
8th	B. Ditchburn
9th	P. Williams
10th	R. Chandler
11th	D. L. Croxford
12th	J. Long
13th	Y. DuHamel
14th	D. Aldana

Fastest Lap: Roberts in 50.8s at 95.67mph
Points: USA — 52. GB — 81.

Race 2
1st	K. Roberts — 17m.22s at 93.28mph
2nd	B. Sheene
3rd	G. Nixon
4th	E. Romero
5th	S. Woods
6th	P. Williams
7th	D. L. Croxford
8th	D. Aldana
9th	J. Long
10th	B. Ditchburn
11th	J. Evans
12th	R. Chandler
13th	G. Fisher

Fastest Lap: Roberts in 50.6s at 96.05mph
(Equals record)
Points: USA — 70. GB — 60.

15th April — Oulton Park
Two races each of 10 laps

Race 1
1st	B. Sheene — 17m.11.8s at 96.34mph
2nd	K. Roberts
3rd	G. Nixon
4th	S. Woods
5th	E. Romero
6th	D. Aldana
7th	B. Ditchburn
8th	J. Long
9th	G. Fisher
10th	P. Williams
11th	D. L. Croxford
12th	A. Baumann
13th	P. H. Tait
14th	M. Grant
15th	R. Chandler

Fastest Lap: Sheene 1m.41s at 98.41mph
(Record)
Points: USA — 74. GB — 61.

Race 2
1st	K. Roberts — 17m.12.0s at 96.32mph
2nd	B. Sheene
3rd	E. Romero
4th	S. Woods
5th	B. Ditchburn
6th	D. Aldana
7th	P. Williams
8th	A. Baumann
9th	J. Long
10th	G. Fisher
11th	J. Evans
12th	M. Grant
13th	D. L. Croxford
14th	R. Chandler
15th	P. H. Tait

Fastest Lap: Roberts and Woods in 1m.41.2s at 98.22mph
Points: USA — 71. GB — 64.
Final Totals: United States — 390 points
Great Britain — 409 points

1974 — How they scored

	Round 1	Round 2	Round 3	Round 4	Round 5	Round 6	Total
GREAT BRITAIN							
P. A. Smart	16	14	14				44
P. Williams	5	8	8	11	7	10	49
D. L. Croxford	11	10	6	10	6	4	47
B. Sheene	14	13	15	15	16	15	88
S. Woods	13	11	12	12	13	13	74
B. Ditchburn	12	9	9	7	10	12	59
M. Grant		2			3	5	10
P. H. Tait	4	1	10		4	2	21
R. Chandler			7	5	2	3	17
	75	68	81	60	61	64	409
UNITED STATES							
K. Roberts	15	15	16	16	15	16	93
G. Fisher	6	4		4	8	7	29
E. Romero	8	6	11	13	12	14	64
J. Long		3	5	8	9	8	33
D. Aldana	10	7	3	9	11	11	51
A. Baumann		5			5	9	19
Y. DuHamel		16	4				20
G. Nixon	9	12	13	14	14		62
J. Evans	7			6		6	19
	55	68	52	70	74	71	390

John Player TransAtlantic Trophy Results   *1975*

30th March — Mallory Park

Race 1 — 20 Laps
1st	K. Roberts	(Yamaha) — 18m.06.6s at 89.45mph
2nd	P. Mahoney	(Yamaha)
3rd	D. Aldana	(Suzuki)
4th	D. Castro	(Yamaha)
5th	D. Croxford	(Norton)
6th	P. Tait	(Yamaha)
7th	J. Newbold	(Suzuki)
8th	S. McLaughlin	(Yamaha)
9th	P. Hennen	(Suzuki)
10th	D. Potter	(Yamaha)
11th	P. McDonald	(Yamaha)
12th	E. Romero	(Yamaha)

Fastest Lap: Roberts in 51.4s at 94.55mph
Points: USA — 71. GB — 55.

Race 2 — 15 Laps
1st	K. Roberts	14m.56.0s at 81.36mph
2nd	D. Aldana	
3rd	E. Romero	
4th	D. Castro	
5th	M. Grant	
6th	B. Ditchburn	(Kawasaki)
7th	P. Mahoney	
8th	D. Potter	
9th	P. Tait	
10th	R. Cleek	(Yamaha)
11th	J. Newbold	
12th	C. Williams	(Yamaha)
13th	S. McLaughlin	
14th	D. Croxford	
15th	P. McDonald	
16th	P. Hennen	

Fastest Lap: Roberts in 58.4s at 83.22mph
Points: USA — 72. GB — 64.

31st March — Oulton Park

Race 1 — 18 Laps
1st	K. Roberts — 23m.23.0s at 76.30mph	
2nd	E. Romero	
3rd	D. Aldana	
4th	S. Woods	(Suzuki)
5th	D. Potter	
6th	B. Ditchburn	
7th	S. Baker	
8th	D. Castro	
9th	S. McLaughlin	
10th	P. H. Tait	
11th	C. Williams	
12th	P. Mahoney	
13th	M. Grant	
14th	P. Hennen	

Fastest Lap: Roberts in 1m.13.8s at 80.68mph
Points: USA — 75. GB — 58.

Race 2 — 15 Laps
1st	S. Woods — 19m.21.8s at 76.87mph
2nd	P. Mahoney
3rd	P. Hennen
4th	D. Castro
5th	S. Baker
6th	M. Grant
7th	D. Potter
8th	P. H. Tait
9th	D. Aldana
10th	P. McDonald
11th	S. McLaughlin
12th	D. L. Croxford

Fastest Lap: Mahoney in 1m.13.4s at 81.12mph
Points: USA — 60. GB — 66.
Final Totals: United States — 278 points
                     Great Britain — 243 points

1975 — How they scored

	Round 1	Round 2	Round 1	Round 2	Total
GREAT BRITAIN					
S. Woods			13	16	29
P. H. Tait	11	8	7	9	35
J. Newbold	10	6			16
M. Grant		12	4	11	27
B. Ditchburn		11	11		22
D. Croxford	12	3		5	20
D. Potter	7	9	12	10	38
P. Mahoney	15	10	5	15	45
C. Williams		5	6		11
	55	64	58	66	243
UNITED STATES					
K. Roberts	16	16	16		48
E. Romero	5	14	15		34
D. Castro	13	13	9	13	48
S. Baker			10	12	22
S. McLaughlin	9	4	8	6	27
P. Hennen	8	1	3	14	26
D. Aldana	14	15	14	8	51
P. McDonald	6	2		7	15
R. Cleek		7			7
	71	72	75	60	278

Photographed during the Liege race of 1974 on his Honda engined Dresda; Dave Degens became the first British advocate of long distance racing. Of a successful home racing background, he certainly succeeded in proving that private enterprise could win over factory cheque books

7 What ever happened to those mice which roared?

Distance racing, that relative term applied in so many different ways, has always provided a vast number of riders with a subtle variation of relief from the otherwise depressing rigours of the more usual short-circuit struggles. The number of events catering for the rider who wishes to pit himself against the generally unrewarding and disappointing struggle against time are not particularly impressive but, where they lack quantity, quality is not in doubt.

No matter what the length of race, riders can generally take things more in their stride, the odd miscalculation now and again not being of such phenomenal importance. The standard of skill, ingenuity and preparation has always been apparent in long distance racing, even from those far off days when the type of machine left much to be desired by modern standards. The impressive improvement of machines is readily apparent and owes a great deal to the testing grounds originally provided by the French and Spanish authorities who were aware, perhaps more so than anyone else, of the important nature of providing the facilities for testing a machine for hour after hour under the most gruelling of conditions. Such events were never designed to make a spectator profit but, unfortunately, the importance of the balance sheet has overtaken the fundamental principles, and what was once a prime requirement of development has now been turned into a sporting attraction second only to the much more variable short distance racing which forms the major portion of the road racer's life. Distance racing is equally important from the point of view that it provides an interested manufacturer with the opportunity to take his prototype machine along to an event and to try it out before going into full scale production. But even this has produced endless political arguments in more recent years, as promoters strove to keep out machines which looked more like thoroughbred road racing machines than the production sports models the events were designed for. The publicity which could be gained from success in these fields was, and is, quite acceptable, so it is little wonder that the definition of an over-the-counter, road-going machine is jealously guarded by some, if not by all. By and large, it has been significant that the people who have gained most from the successes of long distance racing have been the people who have treated the events as proof of their own ability to adapt machines to suit their own personal fancies. At one time these machines used to be referred to as 'bitzas', hybrids built from a variety of components married together to provide either an individual approach to the problem of speed, reliability and handling, or from a commercial standpoint, where a dealer wished to provide himself with a readily available platform from which to launch his own brand of machinery. Both aspects have a place in the modern world of racing, as they had in the past, and people like Paul Dunstall have gained more from their ability to make their own machines than they did from their racing successes. Paul's third place in his first ever race at Brands Hatch on a 500 Dominator Norton in 1958 was just the first step to riches and now his customised Honda and Kawasaki machines have long since outstripped the Dunstall Nortons. The Paris firm of JapAuto have also proved a remarkable success, their rather ugly monster belying its looks by its very obvious reliability. Christian Vilaseca decided that the Honda machines which he sold from his Paris salesroom didn't quite offer the ease of transport that he thought should be made available to his customers and so modified the capacity from 750cc to 969cc by widening the bore, making his own pistons and rings as a consequence and turning out a heavy, almost brutish machine in appearance, but one which has proved remarkably successful both on the race tracks and out of the showroom. Dave Degen's Dresda Autos gave the name to the machine which won Barcelona in 1965, being basically a Triumph Bonneville, so the big manufacturers have not always been

Auzart at Monthlery in 1970

capable of taking one of their own completely standard machines, and winning over those whose ambitions lay in going one better.

The Italian firm of Moto Laverda have also powered through the ranks of manufacturers to become one of the leading exponents in long distance racing in a matter of eight short years. The first year of the Laverda 750 was 1968 when Moto Laverda took part in Motogiro d'Italia, a public road race that has since been cancelled, and won the over 250cc class. Their road racing efforts only started in 1970 when they won the OSS 24 hour race in Holland with the sports model, and came first and third at Monza in the 500 km event, and then won the Zandvoort 6 hour race. With the introduction of the SFC Model in 1971 more success poured their way. In April they were first and second at Imola; in May they were identically placed at Zeltweig in Austria; in June they took the OSS race again and followed with first, third and fourth places at Barcelona. In September Bol d'Or they were disappointed with a second place but snatched a one-two at the Modena 500 km race, final victory at Vallelunga putting them firmly on top of the world.

When in 1973, they withdrew factory teams due to their decision to move to larger premises, they still won the Zandvoort 6 hour race with a machine entered by their Dutch importer. With good placings at home and abroad during 1974 and 1975, this small business has enforced the example that success for a manufacturer does originate from the race circuits of the world. It is an almost unbelievable argument put forward by some manufacturers that racing proves of no benefit. Moto Laverda have disproved this theory in total and remain an example of how to succeed where others fail.

No single chapter can hope to give a true account of the fun and sheer grit which have always been an example of distance racing, whether from the point of view of the rider in the saddle or the mechanics who often toil unmercifully to achieve an outright or even a class win. Every rider believes that he is in with a chance of pulling a win out of the hat; otherwise he wouldn't be there, in the pretty unrewarding world of

Augusto Brettoni partnered by Sergio Angiolini wins the 500km race at Monza in 1970. His machine is a Laverda 750SF

red eyes and oil streaked faces. Class wins, though an acceptable reward, are not as highly prized as the outright trophy, which is probably why more and more emphasis is now placed on the big bikes, rather than the smaller capacity machines which, not so many years ago, used to be a very embarrassing sight way out in front of the field. The modern Superbikes have taken many years to outstrip those diminutive flyers, as we can see from a very brief survey of the world of distance racing.

The category of racing has many faces; from the ultimate twenty-four events, down through the twelve, nine and six hour to the one hour sprints, which, though they cannot be considered within these terms as a long distance race, provide a change from the more usual ritual as we have come to know it. The two-hundred mile events are a relatively new addition for us in Europe and are best left for another chapter, for they are a product of the need to encourage spectators, rather than a foundation for the type of person who wishes to pit his wits and skill against a much more relentless foe — an almost endless goal! The long distance races have a more pertinent problem, that of attracting the public to watch; for in this commercial world in which we now live it is no longer adequate to run what is an expensive event to put on, with little financial reward.

It is also no longer true to say that the event is purely for the riders' enjoyment. The support given to this branch of the sport over the years by the manufacturers, even though late — almost too late — has provided a new interest and spectacle which shouldn't be ignored by the so-called avid followers of motor cycle racing. The pomp and ceremony given to the Le Mans motor race has been applied to the equivalent motorcycling epic, the Bol d'Or, and has largely succeeded. Although gates are increasing throughout the long distance scene, the calendar will not support many races of this nature, and I cannot believe the press figures of spectator attendance at some of the European races, although I am open to correction!

The United States has largely influenced Europe in the 200 mile races, run as either a single race or

Claudio Luigi takes the Vallelunga 500km races for Laverda on board an SFC

divided into two legs, the winner being the one whose aggregate time is the better. This form of racing has been successful in Europe, with Imola leading the field, but it should not go unrecorded that, although American races have produced the revival, the aggregate results system was common many moons ago in Britain.

The oldest of long distance races is probably the Bol d'Or which was first run in 1922 as a twenty-four hour event. It has continued as such to this present day, apart from an almost nine year break from 1960 when it fell into suspension, being reactivated in 1969, and the object of much work and effort ever since to make it the most renowned of all marathons. The concept of long distance racing was not new in England, therefore, when a consortium of the Southampton and Bishops Waltham Clubs, known locally as the Ashton Combine, laid plans for a race of nine hours' duration which would cater for essentially production machines. European events were open to some abuse without serious attempts to maintain a fair balance of equality and the Ashton Combine, led by Neville Goss who, even today, keeps a healthy eye on the road race scene on the FIM, felt that Britain could, and should, offer a similar event. The original scheme was to run a similar twenty-four hour race, but lengthy argument eventually reduced this to just nine hours, a sensible medium distance which would ensure active spectator support. At the same moment the Spanish manufacturers were about to implement a twenty-four hour race over the Montjuich Park roads in Barcelona, but for an entirely different, and commercial reason.

Britain's first nine hour race got off the ground on June 25th 1955 — after the Clubman's TT race in the Isle of Man — on the 2.76 mile Thruxton circuit in Hampshire, the present domicile of Norton Triumph Performance. The arena was to be an ex-Air Ministry site which was usefully converted for use as a motor racing theatre, rather as Haddenham, Ansty and Silverstone had been treated for the benefit of a public who really wanted to steep themselves in the world of Castrol R! The BSA Gold Stars, which had been making

Looking grotesque, the Honda engined JapAuto from Paris was nevertheless quite man enough for the arduous task of long distance racing. This photograph shows two of them before the start of the 1973 Bol D'Or which the firm won

their presence felt in the Clubman's races, proved too strong for the opposition in 1955, the winner's laurels going to Eddie Dow (who has just returned to the scene as the foremost motorcycle commentator in Britain after retiring for two years) and Eddie Crooks, whose prowess with Suzuki during recent years has led to many road race successes, from long distance to TT, to short circuit. Eddie Crooks has recently joined Suzuki GB to superintend their production machine race participation. Surprisingly, 350 "Goldies" won the 1956 and 1957 events where the bigger machines made little impression, but a youthful Mike Hailwood, partnered by near-neighbour Dan Shorey, rode a Triumph Bonneville, entered under the Hailwood Ecurie Sportive banner (For the Love of the Sport), into a well-earned first place, in 1958. The class structure which allowed for a 750cc class for the first three years, was altered to 1000cc that year, and itself subdivided into single and multi cylinder categories. Perhaps a little unfairly this presented somewhat uneven competition as 500cc machines had to compete against the bigger bangers for their class award, as much sought after as the overall win by those aspirants who knew themselves to be in with a chance. Although the first three races were of nine hours' duration, the race was altered, albeit minimally, in 1958, when it became a straight 500 mile race and was renamed the Thruxton 500 Miler, by which name it is commonly known today. Run on a Saturday, the meeting suffered from a lack of spectator potential, which dogged it through future years.

John Lewis and Bruce Daniels broke the British machine dominance in 1959, taking the German 590 BMW to a win, as Bruce did with co-rider Peter Darvill at Montjuich Park, Barcelona, on July 4th and 5th, an event which was to run parallel to the British event for years. At Barcelona, the writing was on the wall, however, for the highly developed Spanish machines finished second, third and fourth — all 125s! The BMW was the first big bike to win. The Bol d'Or that year was a big bike benefit, with Briand and Bargetzi's Norton taking first place from Furling and Merle's BMW. The record distance covered during the twenty-four hours was 1,840 miles at an average of over 76.5 miles per hour, the concept of all distance races based upon the flag dropping after a prescribed number of hours, the winner being the one who had covered the greatest distance.

Imagine then these small machines. The following year 1960, Villa (Franco not Walter) and Balboni took a 175 Ducati into first place and held off the Daniels/Darvill BMW which could but manage second. Third was another Ducati, the average speed 59.25mph covering 603 laps of the 2.35 mile course (1,422 miles). In May, the Vasseur/Maucherat BMW took 1,697 miles to beat the similar machine of Manteau and Larriviere, with a 350 Peugeot in third place. It should be recognised that the Bol d'Or was purely a French national event to which foreign competitors were not invited. Only in recent years has this aspect changed. Small capacity machines sprang up again at the Belgium Warsage 24 hour race, staged over a five and a quarter mile circuit, at the end of July, honours being shared by Heinkel, DKW and Montesa. In the United States, **John Penton was winning the Jack Pine 500** mile endurance run over the Michigan landscape, whilst trials star Ron Langston, partnered by Don Chapman, brought off a surprise win for the Geoff Monty and Dudley-Ward stable at Thruxton on a 650 AJS 31CSR, never reckoned to be the best of roadsters, let alone racing potential. Bonnevilles came second, third and fourth with the Dennis Greenfield/Fred Swift Norton '88' in fifth, taking the 500cc class category from Peter James and *Motor Cycle's* Vic Willoughby riding a Velocette Venom. A 250cc class had been included in 1959 to encourage the development of the smaller capacity machine, particularly in view of the supremacy being shown by the foreign machines, expressly the Spanish whose manufacturers were proved correct in their assessment of long distance racing improving their products. The class was less than a little sparsely populated and a ride-to-work NSU came top, ridden by Alan Pavey and Peter Jordan, two riders of completely different proportions. Southampton's Tony Godfrey won the 1961 race partnered by John Holder, taking race honours back to Triumph and a Honda was entered for the first time, ridden by two Chester riders, Bill Smith and the late MV rider John Hartle. They won the 250cc class against formidable opposition from the latest British two-strokes, Ariel Arrows, ridden by Cecil Sandford, Sammy Miller — yes, Sammy was no mean performer on asphalt — and Peter Inchley, later to take over the Norton Villiers race performance shop at Thruxton! Bernard Moule rode the Fred Warr 883 Harley-Davidson (which I remember used to cost £1 per cubic centimetre) but it holed a piston after meteoric progress from corner to corner. Bob McIntyre failed yet again to win a Thruxton race for Royal Enfield, his series of attempts always ending in disappointment, blow-ups, or crashes. His second place in 1958 on a 692 Super Meteor was his best attempt, but the Redditch company's motto "built like a gun" was to prove too prophetic over succeeding years, even though they built the Constellation for Bob's latter attempts. The semi-works BMW of Darvill again won Barcelona after finishing second in 1960.

1961 also saw the 1,000 km race at Silverstone, a new innovation designed to increase the popularity of production racing. As an event it was supreme, but again a deficit of spectators was experienced, which turned the event into too great a financial risk. It was eventually moved to Oulton Park in 1963 where it died, on a wet and windy day. By the time 1962 broke upon the horizon, Southampton dealer and ex-Norton works teamster Syd Lawton, was set to make production racing history. Syd had always prided himself upon relentless attention to detail, and many a night had gone by when the low drone of his Norton twin could be heard in the gloom of the highways and byeways of Hampshire. You could always tell it was Syd from the once white raincoat he invariably wore. Syd won the next five 500 mile races with a variety of eminent riders. Phil Read and Brian Setchell won in 1962 and 1963, and also added a Silverstone 1,000 km title as well; and Brian, this time partnered by Blackpool's Derek Woodman, took the same machine to victory the following year. Syd changed to a T120R for 1975 ridden by Barcelona winner Dave Degens — who rode his own Dresda to the overall victory — and Syd's son Barry, who was fast learning all about racing on one of his father's Aermacchis. The Norton 650SS "Old Faithful" had managed three seasons and was due for pensioning off. The Triumph was ridden to victory in 1966 by Dave Degens who was this time partnered by Rex Butcher. Triumph machines made it three in a row when Percy Tait and Rodney Gould took 1967 by storm, riding a factory-prepared machine. Percy's only previous success was eleven years earlier when he won the 750cc class on a Triumph entered by Bob Foster. All the big works' machines blew out in 1968 letting Stan Shenton's Boyer Triumph T100T Daytona through to record only the second win by a 500cc machine in the history of the race. Riders were Stan's regular teamsters, Peter Butler and the late David Nixon. Since the 500 miler and, more latterly, the TT and the Hutchinson 100 production races had been carrying the whole theme of production sports machine racing, many other manufacturers had entered into the arena. Suzukis won the 250cc and 500cc classes, the latter with their new Cobra. 1969 saw the return of the Bol d'Or and along with it, the inclusion of the 500 miler in the FIM's newly inaugurated Grand Prix d'Endurance series. The works' Triumph ridden by Percy Tait and Malcolm Uphill led a Triumph walkover, with John Cooper and Steve Jolly second and the Phelps/Carr machine third.

Spanish riders Salvador Canellas and Carlos Rocamara won Barcelona on a 360 Bultaco, ahead of Uphill and Jolly on a Triumph, who were only marginally ahead of Pares and Grav on another Spanish machine, a 250cc Ossa. The prototype category, which had always been a feature of this Spanish classic, allowed many different sorts of machines to take part, and it is interesting to note that the winning Bultaco was classified within this category. A prototype class was the only way in which machines could be raced if they did not conform to the 200 machines manufactured and sold to the public rule, a common restriction imposed to ensure a fair contest. A one hour race was included at Anderstorp, Sweden on August 24th which was again a Triumph benefit. Rod Gould, Percy Tait and Malcolm Uphill filled the first three places. Although this race could not be termed a marathon, it recorded a useful progressive attitude towards production machine racing, and certainly, at the time, help was needed to persuade the world at large that the 500cc World Championship class was not the be-all and end-all of the sport. Production racing had been progressed carefully, much to the credit of Neville Goss, and in 1965 I had the good fortune to persuade my then Board of Directors to run a seventy-five mile race at Silverstone; a race. incidentally, won by Mike Hailwood on Tom Kirby's BSA Spitfire. As John Cooper again proved the following year at Brands Hatch, the BSA left much room for improvment and I was informed, confidentially, afterwards, that many orders were cancelled as a result — a worse handling machine was impossible to imagine! John Cooper was therefore a natural selection for BSA when the time came for the Match Races.

Whereas at home we were enjoying the delights of production racing, in Canada the one to twenty-four hour events had been restricted to endurance tests, letting the records go to Honda when, it appeared, only Honda were on the circuit. The Canadian premiere of the new three-cylinder range was put on at the Harewood Circuit in Ontario in 1968, and proceeded to inject new life into a class of racing that had only been on the go for a couple of years. In August 1968 the Faulds/Murray Honda CB450 won a five hour event from Yvon DuHamel and a chap by the name of Marshall on the inevitable 350 Kawasaki, while a 500 Suzuki was third. The October events provided new interest with the arrival of the 'threes' where they took both production races by storm. In April 1969 Mike Duff, ex-Yamaha teamster and one of the finest riders ever to set foot outside Canada — I rate him far better than DuHamel although he is probably not quite as versatile — took yet another 'three' to victory.

It is an interesting piece of historical fact that it had taken thirteen years for the BSA/Triumph factory to enter officially a team of machines in long distance, and even shorter, production machine races. From a dealer participation point of view, they stood to gain or lose from their involvement, in theory at least, and it was apparent at the time that factories were quite happy to hide behind the cloak and mantle of the Tom Kirbys, Stan Shentons, Paul Dunstalls, Tom Arters, of this world, of whom sport, in the earlier and later 'sixties, was made from, since it was they who provided the drive necessary for production racing to succeed. Even these dealers had to struggle hard for factory co-operation and when, in 1968, the cloak was eventually removed, they had to struggle even harder to get the same optional internals that the factory were found to be using. Private entrants found themselves on the losing end of the scale, which no amount of personal dissatisfaction could dispel. Even Triumph dealers couldn't get some parts, in spite of virtually camping on the Meriden doorstep.

It was, therefore, a prospect which, although perhaps unfair and disproportionate to the true nature of the sport, did kindle the fire of enthusiasm which brought a vast fund of new talent and interest to the progressively drab scene of road racing. Long distance racing was still not interesting enough to invite a captive audience, but the inclusion of works' teams from 1968 onwards was to assist in retaining the overall spectacle of the sport. More star riders became mounted on machines which could be recognised as shop models, and both machine and riders' performances, judged by a very influential and fussy public who appeared quick to react to the results from the circuits. The riders, too, found, by and large, a pleasant change from the hard fought short race battles which formed the entire basis of British racing, earning them the ill-conceived name of scratchers. Scratch they could but their talent was more than that, although their ability to lean on each other continued even in long races!

The ban on double overhead camshaft and rotary disc-valve engines by the FIM in 1969 was retrograde for just one reason — it stifled development of a futuristic design. This was why, in later years, both Bol d'Or in 1970, and the 500 miler incorporated a class for prototype machines for the first time, which allowed experimentation. The British ACU was hopeful that their long considered production racing regulations would be recognised by the FIM at the Autumn Congress, dropping their own badly conceived and very much political regulations which were as far removed from general acceptance as the majority of political divergences. Because

Probably the most famous of all combinations in long distance racing is Godier and Genoud — Alain Genoud here shown riding a 750 Honda at Barcelona in 1974. They now have a Kawasaki contract

we, in Britain, disapproved of the FIM's regulations, we were running the production events as territorial National races and ignoring the unacceptable alternatives. The FIM gave way in the end, but not without a struggle, and the major force for a change came from British sources who could recognise where the sport should be heading even if it didn't always agree upon how it should go about it! The Production TT regulations for 1969 recognised a stable approach to racing, allowing that machines should conform to the 1949 Geneva Convention, even if the manufacturing company had not been party to that convention, and insisting that machines entered should not be more than five years old. Machines eligible had to be registered before March 1st, which arrested the rush to produce a paper figure of 100 machines, the basic requirement of any sports motorcycle eligible for this class of racing. Accountants' certificates, required as proof of manufacture, were not always reliable, particularly in relation to non-British companies.

The 1969 Bol d'Or was won by two young French students, Michel Rougiere, later to race for Harley-Davidson, and Daniel Urdich, on a 750 Honda, hailing from Marseilles. The ride came after both Bill Smith and Tommy Robb had been refused entry to this revived and still closely patriotic French event. Total distance covered was 1740.6 miles at an average of 72.41mph. 500 Kawasakis completed the next three places. Best British machine placing was a Triumph 750 in ninth place. At home the Thruxton 500 miler, which had returned to the Hampshire circuit after a year at Castle Combe, and three years at Brands Hatch crowd seeking, was another Triumph benefit, with Percy Tait and Malcolm Uphill taking the over-all win from the John Cooper/Steve Jolly Triumph.

By the time 1970 dawned upon the scene, a complete reappraisal was taking place on the racing scene over-all, which affected long distance, medium distance and short circuit races alike. A visit to the United States by top British brass towards the end of 1970 brought forth a lot of new ideas to help develop a European attitude that could lead to a stable standard of machine preparation to replace the many anomalies which existed from

The 1975 1000 Laverda 'production racer' which differed from standard in the following major respects – lower frame, 36mm carburettors, camshafts, pistons, gearbox, duplex rear chain, rear disc brake, larger fuel tank, fairing and 3-into-1 exhaust

race to race and from country to country. As the sales potential was highest in America, it naturally followed that the American style of machine classification would suit best of all. This basically insisted upon a standard engine and gearbox layout with few other enforced standardisations. It was upon this premise that in August 1970, Mike Nedham, Director of Engineering at the BSA Triumph Research Station at Umberslade Hall, and I, sat round a few pints and drafted a set of regulations which, with few amendments, were to form the basis of the newly proposed Formula 750 class. Although I don't consider that either of us directed immediate success, we did at least commence the basic paperwork and provided the initial impetus for the type of racing we now enjoy. The new rules were designed to allow scope for experimentation with forks, wheels and brakes along with individual scope for tuning and general machine preparation. If Triumph wished to specify Quaife 5 speed gearboxes, Seeley frames and Fontana forks and brakes, provided the average person could buy them, then the machine in that guise could be used for F750 racing. The new formula was not designed to replace production racing but to augment a new concept of sport with which the public could find some measure of self-recognition.

By 1970 Norton, who had won the Castrol Award for motorcycle design with the Commando, pulled out all the stops and won their own first 500 miler on their own test track. The race, run in the most diabolical weather conditions, was won by Peter Williams and Charlie Sanby in 6 hours 41 mins. 31.4s, no mean average of 74.75mph. Second was the Eddie Crooks-entered Suzuki Cobra, ridden by Stan Woods and Frank Whiteway, while third came the 740 BSA three-cylinder machine ridden virtually in standard trim and giving little advance warning of what was to come! The North West 200 in Northern Ireland found a production class included for the first time, run over Britain's fastest circuit. Welshman Malcolm Uphill totally eclipsed the opposition with a masterly performance on the 650 Bonneville at an average of 106.25mph. Percy Tait was second and Peter Williams third. It was a huge success. Malcolm also took Production TT honours, giving Triumph an unassailable reputation. At the Swedish Grand Prix at Anderstorp in July, a change overcame the racing scene with a win by

Charlie Sanby on the Vincent Davey-entered Kuhn Norton, while Sweden's Bo Granath finished second for Honda and the BMW of Bjorkman was third.

Dave Degens and Ian Goddard stormed the 24 hour race at Barcelona producing the first British win since 1965. Ken Buckmaster rode his 1966 Bonneville into second place and the old twosome of Peter Darvill and Norman Price third with Peter's new mount, the 750 Honda Four.

Although the works' Triumphs missed Anderstorp, they were good enough for a win at the September Bol d'Or with a Triumph three ridden by Paul Smart and Tom Dickie. Always in the hunt at long distance races, Peter Darvill was second with his French co-rider Olivier Chevallier. The Smart/Dickie combination was one of the fastest seen at the Bol d'Or, who had eventually released the French hold on the event and made it a worthy international meeting. To signify the increasing importance and draw of this type of racing, Italians Sergio Angiolini and Agusto Brettoni came third on a Laverda. The 1970 Coupe d'Endurance was won by Peter Darvill.

By 1971, the FIM's Coupe d'Endurance was extended to include Thruxton, Sechsstundenrennen Ostereichring, Barcelona, Zandvoort and Bol d'Or. The Triumph Bonneville was to be replaced by the new three-cylinder machines which had been bench tested as early as January 1965. Although the engine had been planned for quite a time no-one had really given much thought to racing; in fact early use of the machine didn't impress as much as one might have hoped. The bhp was around the 80 mark when a race kitted version eventually ended up on the test bench in 1969; a far cry from the 59bhp of earlier models. A year after the Norton Commando was released in 1967, the threes came onto the market, in March 1968. Their overall visual design was clumsy but there was no doubt that the Hele/Hopwood brainchild was destined to go places by 1971. The T120Rs were fast and beautiful handling machines with the Rob North frame, but their superiority was being challenged. Although both Ray Pickrell and Percy Tait had cocked a leg over a three — Percy succeeded in notching sixth place during the 1969 Hutchinson 100 at Brands Hatch — this was achieved with a basically standard engine. A decision to contest Daytona in 1970 produced a major and significant change in the road racing scene, not only in Britain but also throughout most of the world. BSA/Triumph were going racing and they were intending to win!

Thruxton was again won by a Triumph but this time by a 750 Trident ridden by Tait and Dave Croxford. It was a fortunate win for, with only twenty miles to go, leader Peter Williams dropped the Norton Commando at Cobb Corner. It was a tragedy for the 1970 winning combination of Williams and Sanby, but a situation not unknown to them. Percy's run broke his 650 record set up in 1969, with the 212 laps clocked in 5 hours 54m 26.8s, an average speed four seconds up on his previous best. Barcelona produced a win for the Laverda for the first time, there being no British works entries for the event. Clive Brown and Nigel Rollason succeeded in taking the 500 BSA into second place, ahead of two Laverdas. Smaller capacity machines were suddenly finding it difficult to compete, where once they were dominant. At the Bol d'Or in September there was a considerable works conflict, but Triumph came out on top yet again, with Ray Pickrell and Percy Tait combining to produce a decisive win by seven laps. The machine utilised a 1970 Daytona frame and engine built to full Daytona specifications. Laverda were second and an 850 Guzzi third, ridden by Vittoria Brambrilla and Guido Mancracchi, later to ride the Suzuki of Saaid which was used by Smart and Dickie in winning the 1970 race. The Triumph frame was used by Nixon in the 1970 Race of the Year at Mallory Park. Percy Tait ended 1971 by taking the FIM Award with wins at Thruxton and Le Mans.

Although in 1972 the British and American joint F750 regulations were adopted by FIM as International regulations, it really changed little within the long distance world. But the success of such racing had led to other organisers jumping on the bandwagon. In May, Montlhery staged a 10 hour marathon, won by Georges Fougeray and Jacques Luc on a 750 Honda. The French had become steeped in the tradition of long distance racing as an almost National hobby, for the following year a 1000km event at Le Mans went to the new Kawasaki 750 ridden by Christian Leon and Francois Balde. Second in this race was a 969 JapAuto ridden by Roger Ruiz and Didier Garnier. JapAuto also took the Bol d'Or, beating nearly thirty works' entries from BMW, Moto Guzzi, Ducati, Kawasaki, Yamaha, Suzuki and Honda. The 1973 Bol d'Or was, perhaps the wettest and coldest in the history of the race, Gerard Dubrock and Thierry Tchernine completing 625 laps at 71.87mph, a total distance of 1716.29 miles, lapping around the two minute mark in front of a reported 85,000 crowd. The JapAuto led at the end of each of the six hour periods and, although the 350 Bultaco ridden by Bourgeois and Jimenz did well to finish twelfth, there was no doubt that the big bikes had now come into a world of their own, as well they should, of course.

In the October of 1973, French Champion Jean-Pierre Beltoise won a production race at Montlhery on a 650 Matchless over 43 miles of the concrete track. In April Rouen had catered for 750s with a prize fund of

The breathtaking downhill sweeps of Montjuich Park during the 1975 Barcelona 24 hour race

Spaniard Salvador Canellas en route to victory on his 900 Ducati Desmo, a machine he shared with Benjamin Grau in 1975

£3500, Ron Chandler coming out of obscurity to take the £1600 first prize on a Triumph Trident. This race was split into two one hour races, with the winner decided upon the aggregate results. The previous year Rouen had been the scene of a six hour international meeting which had given victory to two French police patrolmen who achieved the notable distinction of finishing second in both legs of the races. This was also another victory for Kawasaki.

In July 1973, Fabio Taglioni, Ducati's chief designer, saw his 860 vee-twin, ridden by Cannellas and Benjamin Grau, break the Barcelona record by 31 laps, to record yet another of their long string of wins. This machine was entered in the prototype class and proved successful enough to enter subsequently full scale production. In this, the nineteenth annual event, Norton failed to finish, a leaking oil tank taking one and a half hours to repair. Bultaco finished a commendable second, with Du Juan and Alguersuan bringing the 360 machine home into one of its best placings to date amongst the more formidable opposition, and the latest Egli framed Honda was third. Honda was more successful at Spa in August where the two Williams, John and Charlie, covered 280 laps of the Belgian circuit on a machine prepared by ex-Honda boffin Alf Briggs, covering 2450.5 miles in the process and collecting £1000 for their trouble, not that there was any trouble to speak of. The newest Norton 750 was second and the BMW of Jules and Charles Nies third. By this time Norton were seriously considering their effect upon the results of racing, and the opposition, which was gradually making its presence felt. Cosworth were approached to see if they could come up with an answer to the speed and reliability problem, but it was a heartened Norton team who, through the efforts of their number two team of riders, Rex Butcher and Norton mechanic Norman White, slid through to victory at Thruxton.

Yet another long distance race put in an appearance in October of 1973. Amaroo Park, Sydney, Australia, saw the first Castrol six hour race take place which gave Alan Burt's 900 Kawasaki a well deserved win, since he rode the whole of the six hours on his own. A 750 Kawasaki was second, belonging to Warren Willing and Mike Steel, while BMW finished third. The 900 Kawasaki was yet another nail in the coffin of many manufacturers, who had trouble keeping abreast of the times. This 82bhp four cylinder machine was to take no less than forty-six records, world and American, at the Daytona onslaught over the 2½ mile speedbowl. It was voted the *Motor Cycle News* machine of the year, breaking Norton's five year stranglehold. While Norton had always produced a machine of impeccable quality and performance, the latest in the range of Japanese machinery showed progressiveness, power and perpetuity which British manufacturers had difficulty in matching. The new breed of Superbike was a different matter altogether to those Montesas, Bultacos and Ducatis. The 750 Suzuki, announced at the Tokyo Motor Show in 1970, had now been timed at 171.75mph through the Daytona speed trap and this was a performance which none of the existing four-strokes could possibly match. Even a small company like Laverda had their chain driven 980 double overhead camshaft machines, with double disc brakes, rolling off the production line towards the end of 1973. Times had changed quite radically. Yamaha had already announced their 100bhp 500 four which was to be ridden in the world championship races by Saarinen and Kanaya and it wasn't long before the name of Giacomo Agostini was added to the list, changing from the four-stroke MV Agusta to a two-stroke machine for the first time in his life.

1974 was a quite incredible year whether you were interested in long distance racing or the more normal short circuit rituals. There was plenty to interest all avid followers of the sport particularly as, in April, the FIM announced an International ban on the latest of the Yamaha power wagons, the TZ700. The ban wasn't due to hold for long and many organisers just circumnavigated by changing their own rules to ignore the FIM championship and run their event as an open race. In July Kawasaki won Barcelona with Georges Godier and Alain Genoud up while Dave Croxford could but mourn his early lead with his Spanish co-rider Enrique de Juan, which put him up front for the first hour and a half until the crankshaft broke. Ducati took over with Cannellas and Grau until they broke a gearbox. Second was again a JapAuto ridden by Roger Ruiz, this time partnered by Christian Suguet, while Mike Tomkinson's decision to forsake the time honoured BSA gave him third place with Clive Brown and Phil Gurner aboard his Italian Laverda. The first non big bike to finish was fourteenth.

Jean Claude Chemarin and Gerard Debrock dominated the Liege 24 hour race with their 860 Honda. Run over the 8.8 mile Spa circuit, this was the third event in the FIM's Coupe d'Endurance. A chicane had been introduced for the first time to slow riders down which, in a long distance race, was a surprising reflection of the times. Peter Williams had lapped at 133.42mph in July and the organisers were a little wary of the speeds which were likely to result from a repeat performance. John and Charlie Williams' record was broken with the winning pair covering 288 laps at an average of 105.01mph. An Egli-Kawasaki came in second with the Swiss pair of Godier and Genoud in the saddle, names which will never be erased from the history of long-distance racing.

One of the 900 Kawasaki 4s which won the 1975 Coupe d'Endurance Championship

The Le Mans start at Barcelona, typical of the agonising athletic ability needed throughout long distance racing. Following a FIM rule change, this could be the last of the famous runs!

Earlier, over the same circuit, Peter Williams won the 125 mile Formula 750 race for Norton, which was the limit of their success. During the marathon they all broke their primary chains.

The 500 miler was soon no more, its place being taken, in name at least, by the *Motor Cycle* Powerbike International. It was evident that the latest in the breed of Superbikes had become so fast and potent that the name almost personified a new era. With 750cc races being included at meetings such as the Highveld 100 at Kyalami in South Africa, the class was booming throughout the world. No longer could the public, manufacturer and promoter ignore the huge potential from such a sporting class that had almost, by chance, grown overnight. The sheer brutal power was a magnet to rider and spectator alike and even in the long-distance scene, records were being broken as frequently as those during the shorter races, where one expected such a breathtaking exhibition of power and speed. But before Thruxton came the traditional Bol d'Or event, with a repeat win for Genoud and Godier on the four cylinder Kawasaki in an Egli frame. Winners at Barcelona and second home at Spa, they covered 650 laps of the 2.74 mile circuit at 74.50mph. Rene Guili and Gerard Choukroun brought another Kawasaki into second place. It was interesting to note that the first TZ700 Yamahas were entered in this event, complete with lights to get through the night stage. One, ridden by Andre Kaci and Patrick Fernandez, kept going for twelve hours but suffered from an increasing thirst which meant pit stops almost as continuously as the rain which fell.

Kawasaki reeled in yet another victory at Thruxton with the H2R racer, ridden by Barry Ditchburn and South African Kork Ballington. They won by two laps at a record average of 86.33mph, Barry Ditchburn taking the outright motorcycle lap record with him in the process. This win gave Kawasaki their fourth win out of the five International long distance races, and at Thruxton, the first two-stroke win of all time. Triumph machines took second and third place. Pseudo and totally undisguised racing machines were fast stamping their mark on the scene.

In the United States, production races had always been the poor relation to the more glamorous classes, but they took on a new proportion at the Ontario Circuit in May 1974, when AFM staged a 300 mile race which was won by the father and son team of Buddy and Mike Parriott, on board a Yoshimura prepared 903 Kawasaki. The rules allowed virtually anything — as indeed is the case today — and anything really did go! DuHamel's machine sported magnesium wheels but they didn't do him much good! A 900 BMW came into second spot ridden by Bob Endicott and Miles Rossteucher, while Kawasaki were third and a BMW fourth.

Kawasaki had taken most honours in 1974 the world over, rather more so in Europe with major wins at Bol d'Or, Le Mans, Barcelona, Oss, Mettet and Thruxton. In April 1975 they continued their run of success when Godier and Genoud won the 600km race at Zandvoort, but since they refused to have their machine measured after the race they were disqualified from the results, allowing the second team home of Kess Bouweesber and Ryn Kros their first ever win. This event was the first long-distance international race of the season but, although an endurance race, was not to be included in the FIM series which were to comprise the Barcelona, Liege and Thruxton events. While remaining inscribed on the calendar, Zandvoort, 1000km Le Mans and the Bol d'Or were to be ignominious. Georges Godier crashed during the May 1000km Le Mans race and broke his wrist, which effectively removed the favourites. Roger Ruiz and Christian Huguet won the international race with Britain's Dave Potter and Gary Green second on Vincent Davy's Penthouse-entered BMW, though five laps down on the winners at the end of the 226 lap race. The two Spaniards, Canellas and Grau, took Barcelona in July, a fortunate ride for Benjamin Grau since he was originally partnered with Dave Croxford on a Norton entered by the Spanish importer. Neither Croxford nor Grau considered the machine worth riding. First Croxford then Grau refused to ride it in the race and even refused the alternative machine which had been rushed to the circuit. Grau eventually teamed up with Canellas when the works Ducati which Franco Uncini was riding threw him off. With Godier back in action, the favourites for the race were obviously the Swiss pair but a broken main bearing put them right out at the end of the first two hour stint. In spite of their problems, Jacques Luc and Christian Huguet took the Godier/Genoud-prepared 1000cc Kawasaki into second place while Rigal and Chemarin, who retired on the second lap at Le Mans, finished a creditable third.

Ruiz and Huguet took Liege with the JapAuto, providing the second win for the Honda under appalling weather conditions. Italians Roberto Gallina and Nico Cereghini were second on a Laverda 1000, with a similar machine third ridden by Fougeray and Laucchinelli. Godier crashed yet again after twenty-two laps and although suffering no injury, was unable to continue.

At the Bol d'Or on the 20th/21st September, Kawasaki returned with a first, second and third, with the indominitable Godier and Genoud back in the winners' circle. They finished six laps ahead of Christian Estrosi

In brilliant Spanish sunshine, Peter Darvill keeps his Honda 4 ahead of a tight pack of machines all heading for the same spot of tarmac

No time to view the sign posts, this French works Honda rider accelerates away on one of the fast down hill runs in the Montjuich parkland

and Giles Husson, who in turn were two laps ahead of Yvon DuHamel and Jean-Francoise Baldet. The winner's average was 77.329mph for the twenty-four hours. The first three pairs home were all French speaking, a fact which tends to reinforce the domination of the race in an event which they, themselves, started. Almost unbelievably, amongst the whole array of big bikes, Paris motorcycle dealer Eric Offenstadt, himself an old campaigner on both two and four wheels, brought his 375 Yamaha home into seventh place, the first mouse to roar for a long while!

Our own Thruxton 400 the week after provided a change of names with the Luc/Vial Kawasaki (prepared by those brilliant Swiss riders) breaking the record with an average of 87.47mph. Genoud and Godier could only manage a third place on their own machine, which was a position not strong enough for them to retain their FIM title. Chemarin and Rigal took the second place with their 750 Honda and only by hanging on to the German BMW of the Dutch pair Alfred Abfeld and Peter Zettelmeyer could Ruiz and Huguet take fifth place and the overall FIM Coupe d'Endurance for 1975. The Paris firm of JapAuto had succeeded in taking the highest honours in long distance racing.

Although I have made an attempt to provide an interesting breakdown of big bike racing as it has affected the longer distance races, a diary of this nature is incomplete without a working understanding of the difference between the short circuit scratchers and the genuine long distance plodders, like the famous and successful Swiss pair of Godier and Genoud. Techniques vary from team to team, but the underlying principle is one of meticulous preparation and pit work, not to say the design and manufacture of the original machine. To stand up to twenty-four hours of gruelling speed and hammering requires a machine of undeniable stature, and what has been proved over the last decade and, more particularly, over the last few years, is that not one, but a number of machines are all capable of winning. The shorter the race, the quicker people tend to go, and although there are very obvious specialists in the world of long distance racing, shunning the general rat-race of short circuit events, the better of the short circuit scratchers have put in some very impressive performances. Off-hand I can think of few world stars who have even attempted a twenty-four hour event, which must prove something at least — if only that they have little time to pull such an event into their already crowded calendar!

One other fact is worthy of note, particularly as it has been due entirely to the mood of the racing world over the last five or more years. You may wonder why racing machines like the TZ700 and the H2R Kawasaki were allowed to enter the world of long distance racing as they didn't really qualify as a prototype or as an over-the-counter, ride-to-work model. The answer is quite simple. When Britain and America originally agreed upon a set of rules for Formula 750 racing — using as a basis the American system which had been a tried and proven process — they based the foundation upon machines which were manufactured and sold to the public in quantity. This reduced the standard of competition to a level which was entirely acceptable to all, as it brought the cost down to one which would not necessarily break too many bank balances. The machine raced had to be one which used the original engine, gearbox, frame and certain other component parts. Manufacturers, well aware of the opportunity to develop a new market, thus gradually introduced machines of the super-sporting type which were eligible for racing in America and Britain. Eventually the machines turned into a new breed of motorcycle which were available for anyone to purchase if they so wished. Smaller manufacturers who could not compete with the number of machines which they legally had to have available for purchase, rightly complained that even 100 was beyond their ability. MV Agusta, for example, were keen to try out their 750 which was not a brilliant example of their undisputed engineering ability, but would not manufacture a quantity until the orignal proto-type had been perfected. Never keen on long distance racing — in fact they have never taken part in any — they looked to the new 200 milers to provide a launching pad. JapAuto were very much in the same boat, so it was with a degree of satisfaction that they saw the number of machines manufactured and made available to the public drop from 100 to a mere 25. This reduction arrived too late for MV to prepare for 1975, but 1976 may well see the 750 make an appearance on the world's circuits, although I personally doubt that they will want to take in the Coupe d'Endurance series. Within this list of machines appeared the special works' machines; machines like the H2R Kawasaki and the TZ750 Yamaha which were the logical result of a basic production unit being worked upon to produce the ultimate racer within the confines of the rules. That the various factories were quite good at it is apparent from the results. But it would be foolish to accept that there is very much of a completely standard nature within the walls of the major components. All the regulations have succeeded in achieving is what the manufacturer wanted all along — identification with road machines. The Manx Norton, G50 Matchless and the whole string of Honda and Suzuki racers were thoroughbred racing machines. Some of them you could buy and some of them you couldn't with a king's ransom. Now you can, as part of the deal, and although the price may be considered to be too excessive for many pockets, I don't personally feel that the time is ripe to restrict performance and speed by limiting the cost of the machine, as has been the basic formula of some forms of production saloon car racing. Perhaps, in time, it may have some foundation, but both spectators and manufacturers are thriving on the new system and class so there is no need to look anew at the scene just yet.

There can be few people who have discovered no benefit from this latest form of racing. Lessons learned from the race circuits have been converted for use in road machines, with the obvious result that the big bikes in the showrooms today are a combination of engineering theory and practice unrivalled in history. There can be great satisfaction in the average rider knowing that his machine is not so far removed from those seen on the world's circuits, whether on the long-distance tracks or on the shorter British and European ones. The results which he will see chalked up from time to time are proof that he has racing to thank.

Estrosi in action

1975 Coupe d'Endurance — Finishing order

Riders	*Machine*
A. Genoud/G. Godier	Kawasaki
C. Huguet/R. Ruiz	JapAuto
B. Grau/S. Canellas/V. Ferrari	Ducati
J. Luc/A. Vial	Kawasaki
M. Cereguini/Gallina/Brettoni	Laverda
J.-C. Chemarin/H. Rigal	Honda
C. Estrosi/G. Husson	Kawasaki
A. Albfeld/P. Zettelmeyer	BMW
G. Fougeray/M. Luchinelli	Laverda
J. Buytaert/M. Stinglhamber	Honda
G. Green/D. Degens/D. Potter	BMW/Dresda
R. Romeri/A. Sciaresa	Guzzi
J.-F. Balde/Y. DuHamel	Kawasaki
H. Dahne/R. Guili	BMW
J.-B. Peyre/D. Ravel	Kawasaki
C. Bourgeois/G. Mandracci	JapAuto
J.-P. Boinet/G. Debrock	Yamaha
R. Newby/J. Strijbis	Triumph
E. Elias/S. Heltai	Kawasaki
J.-C. Meiland/Terras	Kawasaki
J.-J. Coq/E. Offenstadt	SMAC
Dickie/Pendlebury	BMW
J.-P. Bertsch/G. Maison	Honda
S. Parrish/C. Revett	Suzuki
R. Millet/J.-M. Torres	Ducati
F. Fiasconi/G.-C. Pelatti	Ducati
F. Exelman/Ph. Wybo	Kawasaki
G. Bougard/R. Mullender	Kawasaki
R. Marshall/P. Tait	Suzuki
Glauser/Wenger	Honda
G. Ermanno/C. Santarelli	Ducati
J.-C. Meunier/C. Meunier	Ducati
A. Sorci/G. Valli	Segoni
D. Endean/B. Seward	Suzuki

8 For the sake of its feet a horse was lost

The modern concept of a road or racing tyre is oh, so different from that conceived by John Boyd Dunlop in what we now like to term those 'pioneer' days of motorcycling. Times really have changed and with them the design of the tyre; and yet the original principle of rubber filled with air hasn't changed from that day to this, although some will remember riding on solid tyres before the air we breath was harnessed to provide the earliest form of suspension! That must have been something to remember!

Since the original racing machine had to be standard and thus the tyres as well, you could say that both tyre and machine have developed together along an identical road. Perhaps the tyre manufacturer has always had to help solve the engine and frame designer's ultimate problems, but the consistency of parallel development has produced a total product in which neither is more efficient than the other, accepting that perfection can never be achieved. The tyre has always borne the brunt of inadequate frame design, engines with great torque, and the variety of stresses under braking and cornering. It must be accepted that the motorcycle is a design like no other in that it is the total balance of machine and rider under every given circumstance that makes it so much fun — and so much of a problem for the designer, whose whole outlook must eventually regard safety as a major factor.

Few roads are straight, even fewer are flat with an even surface, and few countries in the world have a consistent climate. Imagine the problems in Britain and Europe where the weather can change constantly from hour to hour, let alone from day to day. The European motorcyclist rides and races under all weather conditions —all, that is, but under suicidal conditions — so the tyre designer has to take every factor into consideration when he produces a tyre with a particular profile, tread and compound. Imagine the situation in the Isle of Man TT where thirty-seven and three-quarters of a mile can vary from wet, dry, damp, thick fog and ice — almost all in one lap. Maybe it is a slight exaggeration, but certainly I have witnessed conditions which, in the pub afterwards, aren't so far out at that!

Riding on the road and on the race track are now two totally different things although road tyres have greatly benefitted from racing knowledge. Ten years ago they were very similar in a lot of respects and it is interesting to note the technical similarities.

A flat tread is out of the question for two wheels as the profile shape of a tyre must, of necessity, ensure that the maximum amount of rubber is kept on the road at all times; and when a motorcycle leans into a corner it would present only a thin ridge contact to grip the road. For many years a round tread section was most favoured, which allowed for a reasonably flat contact area to form between the tyre and the road at all attitudes of the machine. The higher speeds which have been developing over the years have presented the problem of transmitting the horse power of the engine to the grip at the rear wheel, and the performance figures which Dunlop have produced from time to time show that the average 750cc motorcycle possesses powers of acceleration considerably in excess of any sports car on the market. This power is intensified because, unlike a car, the motor cycle has only two wheels against twice that number; when the three cylinder BSA/Triumph came onto the scene the problems involved in harnessing the power to weight ratios became an immediately urgent problem, which had to be solved, particularly in view of the fact that the racing versions were to become so successful against far mightier opposition.

In the late 1950s, during tyre testing with Bob McIntyre at Oulton Park, using the old round profile tyres, the Dunlop development team noticed that wear was taking place mainly on the shoulders of the tyre whereas the centre tread area remained virtually unworn. Dismissing this as not being a sign of underinflation — a problem

KR 108 front slick

Dunlop KR 111 rear slick about which, at present, there is so much controversy

KR 83 Dunlop showing the grip cells. This tyre was developed from MV's testing

known to the average road going motorcyclist of my generation at least — this led the Dunlop designers to consider that a racing machine, when leant over, required more contact area at the shoulder to counteract the very high slip forces, and when vertical, a compromise was required to provide sufficient contact areas for accelera- tion and braking, and yet little enough to keep rolling resistance to a minimum. The designers came up with the triangular section tyre, or trigonic, to give it the correct definition, but this was not entirely popular throughout the racing world. Riders of slightly less stature came to the rapid conclusion that they couldn't race on them. No longer could you gently roll into a corner as you either had to be upright or right over, as the case presented itself. Of course, for the better quality of rider these tyres proved of immense advantage, particularly on British short circuits; but the general run of the mill competitor reverted to Avon tyres, for long Dunlop's only real competitor in Europe, and were quite happy to use the standard road tyre on which they felt a lot safer and which cost them surprisingly little. The Avon Rubber Company, who had pulled out of racing in 1962, had stopped manufactur- ing their highly popular racing tyres, which riders bought up in quantity when they realised that their only alternative was the triangular Dunlop. The trigonic tyre was designed for racing in 1961 and produced a consider- able increase in safe cornering speed. It was at first known simply as the 'triangular', later as the Dunlop RMT1 and later still as the KR73 (road version). This tyre suited the BSA/Triumph triples to a 'T' as it provided a broad flat contact area when cornering that allowed high speeds to be obtained in safety. The tread pattern life how- ever, although ample for races, was not long enough for the ordinary rider and hit his pocket a little too hard. As a consequence a design half-way between the triangular profile of the racing tyre and the then normal road tyre was considered best suited for the average road rider, and the K81 Roadmaster trigonic tyre was introduced onto the market. The standard K70 tyre was about 107% squat; the section height was 7% greater than the width. This was unsuitable for high speed work because it promoted lateral instability and roll. The trigonic was designed to be 90% squat. The design of the tread pattern allowed for the additional weight of the 'threes' and incorporated structural features in tread pattern and casing which promoted safety under any circumstance.

From the introduction of the 'triangular' racing tyre and Avon's tragic demise from the road racing scene, Dunlop became king of the racing circuits. The lack of competition between rival manufacturers, so often the death knoll of an industry, little affected development of the racing tyre, as increasing speeds, plus the sheer

The American team kitted out themselves well with Goodyear tyres at the Easter Match Race 1976, and even got down to hand cut slicks

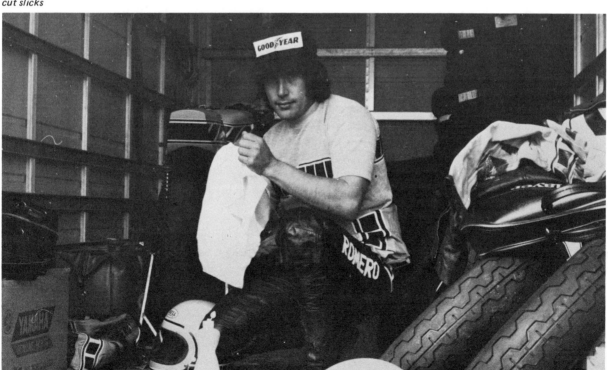

torque being developed by the new breed of 750cc machines, was competition enough on which to dwell. The
high hysteresis or 'sticky' tyre compounds were developed and, in conjunction, an ultra competitive road-cum-
production racing tyre was manufactured, which was originally designated the K81 and then renamed the TT100
after Malcolm Uphill's Isle of Man lap in 1969. This new tyre gave excellent road performance but would never
act as a double 'agent'. It was superb on the track and road but was not much good on rougher surfaces met by
motorcyclists the world over. Incidentally, it was at about this period that the old concept about using ribbed
tyres on the front wheel and the transverse grooved rear tyre was dispelled. The circumferential grooves on the
front tyre were designed to resist side slip and the transverse slots on the rear to facilitate acceleration and
braking. However, increased knowledge about grip in the wet, coupled with the consecant curve principle of tread
pattern design, led everyone to the conclusion that the ideal tread pattern design for both front and rear wheels
was one which was universal to both. The performance of the TT100 amply upheld this conclusion.

With the introduction of the Formula 750 in the United States and Europe and the increasing power demanded of the 500cc world championship machines, the triangular profile tyres, even with their later grip cells,
developed for MV Agusta, had reached the end of their development. Machines had become heavier and more
difficult to control and thus the transition from upright to banked position, once the bane of the amateur's
existence, had to be more gradual, if riders were to develop anything less than Herculian muscles. The handling
of these big bikes was generally inferior to the smaller, nippier machines, which called for a new riding technique
which did not suit the triangular principle. Rounder profile tyres, were once again reverted to for the big bikes
but with a decade of experience of rubber compounds and tread patterns. Smaller machines found more
advantage in the triangulars.

During 1970 and 1971, Dunlop had extended its sphere of influence into the United States, firstly with the
introduction of the BSA/Triumph triples, into an arena ruled for so long by Goodyear, who had never been
convinced that their involvement with two wheels could be all that rewarding. In a short period Dunlop swept
the board, culminating with seven wins out of the eight possible Grand National races in the 1972 calendar and
a clean sweep the following year. Michelin entered the racing scene by introducing the completely 'bald' treadless
tyre known as the 'slick', an approach followed closely by Dunlop and Goodyear. The 'slick' was nothing new
and had been successfully employed in sprinting for years on the basis that the more tread on the road the more
adhesion. Avon had produced one-off sets for George Brown a decade before. What was new was its employ in
racing, where the rounded section was totally different to the almost cross-ply section of the sprint tyre, with
its heavily supported walls. In 1974 and 1975 Dunlop successfully produced the tyres that took Phil Read (MV)
and Giacomo Agostini (Yamaha) to victory in the senior world championship, while the basic trigonic racing
tyre helped Walter Villa and Johnny Cecotto to the two smaller capacity championships.

Tyres have been very much in the news quite recently due to the fact that the Dunlop, Goodyear and
Michelin 'slicks', designed to ensure total adhesion to the road in the dry, leave much to be desired in damp and
even wet weather conditions where they are almost fatal. Even in the dry at Daytona, Barry Sheene was lucky to
escape his quite rapid prang when a rear 'slick' gave out on him, and Mick Grant too, was thankful that the Gods
were with him in a similar escapade later in the year at Ontario. During the Easter Match Races, the poor
conditions at Mallory Park, where snow started half way through the first race, were enough to send everyone
searching for the more normal treaded tyres before the second race, but the fact remained that even the so-called
'intermediates' — hand cut slicks to provide at least three water channels — were not good enough to provide any
great degree of safety. Only the old fashioned treaded tyre would have withstood competitive racing, the tyre
about which John Surtees once remarked, "could cut its way through a lake". But the desire to be competitive
is the biggest danger factor. Argument is bound to be quite strong both for and against. There is no question that
slicks in the dry are as safe as any other tyre in the world. The fact that their design and manufacture is pushed
to the ultimate in this present day world of the 180mph machines is not the basic bone of contention, although
even in this area some of the faster of the world's circuits are being banned from staging world championship
events unless chicanes are introduced to slow artificially the progress of these big bikes. What is at debate is the
effect of damp or wet weather after a race has started, where riding can be likened to skating on a very fine sheet
of ice. Under these circumstances, is it correct to let racing continue or must organisers use their own powers to stop
the race? — all because of the wrong type of tyres for the conditions. Motor sport has the same problems, although
the alternative in a Grand Prix is to stop and change wheels, a gamble that may or may not prove successful; rather
the same as a dubious choice of tyres before the start of a motorcycle Grand Prix where the weather may not be
settled. Accept one thing for certain. If the race does stay dry and a rider has opted for treaded tyres, there is no

Don Castro at speed at Talledega showing off the slicks to good advantage

way that he is going to win against others on slicks. That the reverse also applies under wet conditions is the danger of allowing the riders the choice of tyre. At least a car can have its wheels changed in a matter of seconds. The motorcycle racer, once the decision is made, has only one alternative to riding on — and that is to retire from the race and with that retirement may go his hopes of a championship.

The smaller capacity machines have continued to take advantage of the trigonic tyres as their smaller stature allows for better handling than the almost overpowered big bikes on the world's circuits today. A 750cc machine landing after the take-off from Ballaugh Bridge in the Isle of Man puts collossal forces on the casing and tread. On the banking at Daytona the force of the machine depresses the suspension and, eventually, the tyre, with consequent high temperatures building up through the early part of the race. It should be little wonder that accidents happen under such circumstances, but more of a wonder that they do not happen more often. It is a great tribute to the tyre manufacturer that his knowledge is more than capable of keeping machines on the road no matter what they have to do, and the horse power can be shod with the right sort of steel!

The choice of tyres is one of personal assessment. Pat Mahoney chooses Michelin and Sheene, on this occasion, Dunlop

9 Johnny who?

The style which made him famous the world over and which led to his outstanding success in 1975

Quietly awaiting the start of the Hutchinson 100

For a man to come out of almost total obscurity to win a world title in one season is nothing short of amazing. For the same man to win the complete respect of every other rider is also quite an incredible feat, but such a man is Alberto Cecotto, nicknamed Johnny by his father. Overnight sensations are more usually found in show-business rather than on the world's racing circuits, so it was with more than a little alarm that riders at Daytona looked at the performance of this newcomer to the scene. In a sport which demands the highest of skills and not just nerve alone, newcomers have always had the habit of disappearing into ignominity rather quickly. Some have even parted the way of all flesh after a very short flourish in which their rise to stardom had the anticipated conclusion. "I told you he wouldn't last", is a common remark all too often heard and all too often proven correct.

But the name of Johnny Cecotto has remained indelible throughout 1975. He has proven that stars can be born with a natural ability to master two wheels in a very short period of time. He had the background, for his father, Giovanni, had himself won the Venezuelan championship on a Manx Norton in the middle fifties and had bought his youngest son — there was another Cecotto on the scene already — a 750 Honda four in 1972. Johnny raced this machine twice, taking a first and a second place in his open class against allcomers. His surprise performance was enough to interest the Kawasaki importer who gave the youngster a three cylinder 750 to race.

"It was more enthusiasm and determination rather than ability that carried me through in those days", remembers Johnny. "At one meeting at Interlagos in Brazil — it was a 500 mile race — I crashed heavily after pulling through the field to third place after a very poor start. The first aid men wanted me to go hospital for a check-up but I tore myself free of their clutches, picked up the bike and rejoined the race." The crowd loved it of course and when Johnny regained his third place they went wild with glee.

For a moment you would think that they were brothers! In fact Jose Cecotto is out on the circuit in front of a sun drenched Brands Hatch crowd

The races on the Honda and Kawasaki could be counted on the fingers of one hand, for it did not take long before the Venezuelan Yamaha importer, Andres Ippolito, was taking an interest in this amazing youngster. By 1973 young Cecotto was racing a 350 Yamaha and winning Venezuela's eight road race meetings a year. In both 1973 and 1974 he took the 1000cc championships. His one big love, though, was big bikes.

"I suppose it is because I started on big bikes that I enjoy them so much," Johnny recalls after one of the finest seasons in the lives of any rider. Not surprisingly Johnny was keen to try Daytona on a 750. He had ridden at Daytona in 1974 on the 350 but was placed a lowly thirty-fifth. Perhaps only one person was not surprised by his immediate success which left the Suzuki camp wondering who this bloke was. His third place is already written into the history books for, unlike others of Latin temperament — both his parents emigrated to South America from Italy — his was not a race for ultimate glory; a sort of do or die affair which has proven to be so disastrous for some of the most promising riders. He rode a fine, well-judged race from the back of the third wave of riders and impressed everyone who witnessed the progressive ability of this nineteen year old. Most wondered if it could survive disaster.

A few weeks later he rode his second race on the 750 at Imola. He won, but by this time the win came as no surprise because, in between times, he had taken the French Grand Prix by storm winning both 250 and 350 classes. In 1974 he rode a 700 Yamaha at Imola but the engine packed up after only a handful of laps. 1975 was a different story, and after setting a cool practice reputation he demolished the field in the two one hundred mile races. Of all the machines he has ridden Cecotto still loves the big bikes. "The power is always available and they handle well."

This youngster from Caracas is going places in 1976. His broken foot came at the end of the 1975 season when there was little left to race for. He missed the Race of the Year, much to the disappointment of the British crowds, who had already had a foretaste of his prowess at the Silverstone meeting and the Hutchinson 100 at Brands Hatch. The incident therefore drew his racing season in Europe to a slightly premature closure. Venezuela went mad over Cecotto. The T-shirts and haircuts have been modelled on this youngster who has the world — and the women — at his fingertips. And yet he remains slightly modest in all but Barry Sheene's company. It makes you wonder what would happen to the world if Sheene, Cecotto, Aldana and Romero were left in charge! I doubt that there would be much of it left. Like Fangio and Fittipaldi, Cecotto has come out of the relatively unknown blue of South America. Unlike Caldarella, it doesn't look as though he will retreat very quickly and he puts the learning of English high on his list of ambitions. When and if the Formula 750 championship accedes to world championship status "Johnny" Alberto Cecotto will be young enough to take the title to South America.

10 Defeat of a legend

It is a unique piece of racing history that a machine which was destined to succeed on race circuits the world over, was to eventually fail through no fault of its own, its riders, designers or mechanics. We talk, of course, about the BSA and Triumph triples which brought a new sight and sound in 1971 to the merriment of rider and spectator alike. The howl of the threes was a joy to listen to and the reliability and sheer speed of these four-strokes renewed our faith in the British manufacturer. That it didn't last doesn't detract from the memory of a machine that made it to the top in a couple of very short seasons and which, for me at least, produced one of the most resounding successes in the history of motor cycle sport.

But to paint a picture of the race and the aftermath we have to consider a little background. The three-cylinder machines from Birmingham and Meriden were designed as road bikes to meet a growing market for big machines in the United States. In fact, I seem to remember that the home market was severely rationed in 1970, both for such machines and, almost as important, the spares to go with them. Bench tested to 80bhp late in 1969 they gave an indication that, in racing trim, they could successfully compete on American circuits. Regardless of the arguments to the contrary, racing success does help to sell machines so it was a facet that could not be ignored. Triumph in Britain had produced some remarkable results with the 650 Bonnevilles and it was a moot point whether or not the threes would be better than the tried and tested mounts. In charge of the racing programme was Doug Hele, transported during earlier years from the Bracebridge Street Norton empire, not too unlike the great Joe Craig in temperament and attitude. Always careful not to give away too much from his countenance, Doug had already become a bit of an enigma in the world of motor cycle racing. His engineering background had always been motorcycles, apart from his apprentice days with Austin Motors, now part of the British Leyland group, at Longbridge. With designer Bert Hopwood, the man who designed the three, Doug made the racing work and with Rob North, who designed the racing frame to go round the power-house, was predominantly responsible for its success on the circuits. Percy Tait, Triumph's main test rider and a man who had (and still has, come to that) lost his birth certificate, took the first machine to Elvington aerodrome, recording a mean average of 157mph, faster than the 650s and the 750 twin the year before. In December 1969 it was decided to build six machines for Daytona — in March 1970 — which gave little time for testing or for ironing out the many problems which always beset new models. In fact, the first machines had a design fault in the steering head of three degrees which affected their handling, but new frames were built after Daytona and the Fontana front brakes later gave way to twin discs for 1971.

With his superb riding of Tom Kirby's unofficial works BSA at Silverstone and Brands Hatch during the now famed production races in the Hutchinson 100 (for which yours truly takes all the credit) Derbyshire ace John Cooper assumed a natural claim to ride a three in the first of the Match Races, even though his choice was not universally approved by the BSA/Triumph group. John had always been outspoken and if he felt that the spade really was the proverbial bloody shovel he usually said so, tempered with his own particular brand of good humour — of course! It had always been John's ambition to race big bikes, his more usual machinery being 250 and 350 Yamahas and the 500 Seeley on which his fame was at its highest, no more so than at Mallory Park where the Master of Mallory reigned almost supreme.

"Norton's and the rest were almost like vintage machinery by the time I rode the three," commented John, when forced to remember back to the time he first cocked a leg over one. "The BSAs, with new suspension, new tyres and plenty of power, were obviously the thing to race and, surprisingly, I found them easier to ride.

John Cooper on his earlier winning way astride Tom Kirby's BSA Spitfire

You had to concentrate more because they were faster but I took to them straight away.'' But John's first outing was almost his last as the story of the Match Races has already outlined. He asked the factory officials, particularly Peter Deverall and Doug Hele, if he could race the BSA again but they replied that with riders like Paul Smart, Ray Pickrell, Percy Tait and Tony Jefferies they did not need anyone else nor had they, for that matter, any spare machines.

As the weeks rolled past and the Race of the Year at Mallory Park loomed nearer, John thought more and more that the BSA was the machine he needed for the Leicestershire event, perhaps the finest single piece of high speed entertainment seen on the British mainland. He had already won the event twice previously; in 1965 on a Norton and the year of 1970 riding his own framed Yamaha, the Yamsel, a special lowslung lightweight model of the 350.

''I asked Doug Hele who was in charge of the team if I could have a test ride on the bike before the Race of the Year as I thought that the machines were not being ridden to capacity.'' Faced with that sort of attitude it was no wonder that Doug turned the request down but that was, after all, the John Cooper everyone knew. Thinking things over John didn't give up hope and decided to speak to Peter Deverall, Marketing Director. He told him of his conversation with Doug Hele and asked him if he (Deverall) could change his mind. ''If you give me a bike I will win the Race of the Year for BSA,'' claimed John, which he now admits was rather a big statement and rather stupid at the time. He had raced the bike only three times before during the previous Easter with inconspicuous success so he was lucky that his rather bland statement was taken seriously. But it was taken seriously, more so for this one event than any other, for John was supreme at Mallory Park and more than anything else BSA needed the prestige from a home win in front of Britain's biggest motorcycle crowd. If anyone could win at Mallory Park it had to be John, for neither Paul, Ray, Percy nor Tony could hope to match the inconquerable Cooper round the tight 1.35 mile circuit.

The bike chosen for John was almost brand new and the Thursday before the Sunday race John got to try it out for the first time. After four laps he was consistently lapping at record speed but though it was geared the

Cooper in action on the BSA Rocket Three, seen here at Mallory Park in that famous encounter which had the crowds cheering as never before

same as the other works machines for Mallory, John felt it was very much undergeared for the race itself. No sprockets were available, so it was Saturday practice before the new gearing could be employed. It suddenly became obvious that the Cooper/BSA combination was going to take some holding and Mike Hailwood was there to witness just how quick he was.

Before the race had started there was some controversy as to what type of start it was going to be. Agostini had seen the pace of the triple in practice and though under normal circumstances he wouldn't have worried too much what sort of start he had to make, the sudden threat of a British 750 made him insist on a push start.

"The BSAs were very, very hard to push start," remembers John, who was a little concerned to bring his boast to fruition. Agostini himself was no sluggard at Mallory, having won in 1966 and 1969, and the MV Agusta was almost the perfect machine. Surtees, Hocking and Hailwood had romped the MV home to superb wins since the initial event in 1958, and its ease of push starting was a legend in itself. "You had to reach maybe ten miles an hour with the BSA before you leapt on board. If it fired you were well away but if it didn't you had to start all over again." John must remember those days vividly because the advent of the triple on British circuits changed the starting rules and allowed organisers the option of clutch or push start. In point of fact we, in this country, did what the Italians always did to us: we ignored the FIM rules which only allowed clutch starts for sidecar events at International meetings!

From the start John was fifth into Gerards, three down on Agostini. By the Esses, Cooper had closed on the Italian who moved into the lead on the back straight. No-one was taking any chances in this race for, apart from all the normal International stars, the legendary Mike Hailwood was back in action on a works Yamaha. After a few laps the two were locked in combat with the wily Cooper staying with the fleet Italian. "He was in trouble round Gerards and I was in trouble at the Esses" says John. "As that virtually equalled things up the race settled down a bit and I was able to nip ahead of him at the Esses." What John does not record was the almost unbelievable reaction of the crowd who stood up and cheered to a man. The crowd was in a panic of excitement. There were hundreds of people on top of buildings, up trees, on the signboards, and almost as many on the roof of the

Big money in America — John Cooper holds £5,000 worth of cheques he gained for his win at the big Champion Spark Plug Classic at Ontario in 1971

main grandstand as there were inside. Mallory was alight from tip to toe. "He took the lead back again and from then on it was a race long dice. He got into a slide at Gerards and I had a big moment at the Esses and after about twenty laps I took the lead again for the last time. It was fantastic, really great, and easily the most enjoyable race I have ever ridden in. The bikes were dead equal. The MV was just a little bit quicker than the BSA out of the hairpin, but down the back straight they were about the same," says John. But how did John manage to claim final victory?

"In one of the races before the main Race of the Year someone had fallen off at the Hairpin and dropped a load of oil right on the normal racing line. Although it had been cleaned up, it was still a bit on the slippery side and Ago, with the very low bottom gear, had to stay on a very tight line, while I had to go wider with a higher bottom gear. This again levelled us up, making so much of a race of it. But on the last lap I decided I would take the inside line because this corner seemed about the best place for Ago to retake the lead, by my going wide and him diving up the inside with that neat little bottom gear pull away which could leave anyone standing. I stayed in front and left him with no chance at all."

Photographic proof of the fact that 'JC' suffered his moments of agony in chasing the illusive Ago!

One of John's best rewards of the day was not the £1000 guineas cheque nor the acclaim of the crowd. It was the remark of Doug Hele who said that he hadn't realised that John was such a good rider! John had achieved his boast and had beaten the great Agostini, then at the pinnacle of his prowess on the 500 MV. It was one of the great races of all time and certainly one which put the Superbikes on the map. It was a defeat which was difficult to bear and even more difficult to believe when it happened a second time — at Brands Hatch during the traditional Race of the South in October.

For the Mallory Park meeting John had raced the triple with standard, high-compression pistons, but, fired with success at Mallory Park, Doug Hele rushed back to the factory to find even more power. "I said we didn't need any more," said John ... "but Doug said we did, so that was that." By coincidence John bumped into Ago at the hotel. "I've got a new engine for this race," said Ago. "That's funny," returned John, "so have I." The psychological adventure had started with the first round to JC. The race itself was a walkover for the BSA, with Ago trailing home about one hundred yards behind. It was demoralising for the MV factory who, though they gave away 250cc, felt that their sportsmanship had lasted long enough. It was a long time before the 500 MV was to compete against bigger capacity machines again.

Just to put the cap on the season Cooper and the BSA were packed off to Ontario for the Champion Spark Plug Classic. This was a far cry from the British short circuit and needed a lot of heart searching before a decision was made to compete. It was virtually accepted that the only real chance they had was to run through each leg without refuelling, the seconds gained going to compensate towards the loss of speed handed to the big Kawasakis and Suzukis, and even the 350 Yamahas. Careful calculations showed that the BSA could, in fact, run through without a pit stop, but there was still considerable doubt that any gain of time in this direction would be sufficient to overcome the brutish power of the Kawasakis. With Cooper's BSA went a machine for Gary Nixon, who had been deprived of a ride at the Race of the Year when his machine was given to Paul Smart. Paul was not to ride at Ontario, for the financial difficulties facing the BSA/Triumph Corporation already meant cutting back on expenses. Fog delayed the arrival of machines and men and John's practice was thus reduced to a minimal amount. Wearing the helmet given to him by Dick Mann who just couldn't believe that anyone would wear such ridiculous headgear as John's low crown 'pudding basin', John finished third in the first race just behind Kel Carruthers on the 350 Yamaha. By the second race John was therefore in a position to finish high up on aggregate but no-one gave him any chance of winning. Fortune smiled when a seven-man pile-up in that second race removed Gary Nixon, Yvon DuHamel, Cal Rayborn and Dave Aldana. That left the tough little Australian Kel Carruthers, ex world champion and the man that had taught the Americans all he knew about racing. The BSA/Triumph team were not very good with their pit signals but John had worked out for himself that he had to beat Carruthers to win overall victory. For twenty of the thirty-eight laps John was all on his own, apart from forgetting that the race started when the flag was lifted! In fact John was lucky not to have been brought down in that oil slick. "It was a boring race, so boring that I had time to watch the light aircraft landing at Ontario airport!" It was this lack of concentration which allowed Carruthers to catch John and pass him, but once Kel was ahead the boredom soon passed, and John was fired up again, and the race was on. Thanks to the lack of pit signals, John had been watching the illuminated scoreboard in the centre of the track for the count-down to the chequered flag but coming into the finishing straight the last lap flag was out with the board showing three laps to go! Carruthers had made twenty yards and there were two tail-enders in between. "Oh God," said John, "This is the final." (Personally, although John claims these were his words, I cannot exactly say that I believe him but I doubt that the truth could be printed anyway!) John got cracking and passed six back markers round the outside of a horseshoe bend close to the finish. He passed another on the next bend and in the run-up to the flag he was still ten yards behind Carruthers. "I slipped into the Yamahas slip-stream and pulled out just before the line to win by four inches." Doug Hele had started walking back to the paddock during the latter stages of that last lap. Over-revving it through the gears had been enough to clinch the largest of victories by the smallest of margins. But the matter-of-fact Cooper wasn't worried that he had almost lost the race by total lapse of concentration. He didn't lose did he! "It's first under t'linen that counts."

In financial trouble, BSA gave John a machine for 1972 and paid a mechanic's wages for the season. But it was entirely a private effort from John's garage business in Derby, and without the factory backing he could not hope to improve the machine in line with the constantly increasing opposition. Even so he won the *Motor Cycle News* Superbike Championship, making it two in a row for the factory. He was a lucky man for in the final round at Brands Hatch he threw the bike away at Paddock Bend, ripping the leathers off his back. The bike was flattened down one side but his mechanic, Steve, ripped off the fairing, straightened the handlebars and John rejoined the race in tenth position. Improving as the twenty-five lapper unfolded he regained the lead and went on to win the title.

Chance of another Race of the Year victory in 1972 wasn't really on the cards after Jarno Saarinen was seen to have entered. With the works Suzukis there, John had to settle for a third place, baulked by Paul Smart at the hairpin on the last lap. The most he could have managed would have been second, for Jarno was out of sight, setting an incredible lap record in the process, on the 350 Yamaha.

John is still full of praise for the triple to this day. "The bike never misfired or stopped once while I was racing it. Once it did 1000 racing miles without even taking the head off" says John. "With more money for development and Doug Hele working on it, the bike could have gone on for at least two more years as a competitive racer. It was only a few miles down on top speed, that's all." John still believes that a six speed gearbox instead of the five gears that it had, plus a few more horses, would have made all the difference in the world. In fact John still claims that there is still a super lightweight 750 BSA lying around in a corner of the factory. He spotted it one day and hoped then that it was for him to ride. It never saw the light of day!

11 Number one–
Gary Scott
Champion's gallery

Gary Scott at Baldwin Park, California, America's new National Champion but did not stay with Harley-Davidson for 1976

When Harley-Davidson lost the title in 1973 to the fleet and highly competitive Yamaha of Kenny Roberts, it looked rather like a spell in the doldrums for Harley-Davidson who, apart from a few years, had made the number one emblem the basis of their advertising since time immemorial. If Harley-Davidson had lost some of their enthusiasm for the American title it would have been hardly surprising, for the loss of Mark Brelsford and Cal Rayborn were blows from which they would not easily recover. The disappointment with the 500 Aermacchi/Harley-Davidson two-stroke was a real set-back to their road racing plans, where they needed a rapid machine to be on even level terms with the mighty two-strokes of Yamaha and Suzuki. But out of the mist arose a new talent, that of Gary Scott, whose continual competition with Kenny Roberts has set something of a record in American racing. It began in 1970 when Roberts beat him for top honours in the Novice Class and then followed it up by another defeat in 1971 when Scott was again runner-up for Junior honours. Gary Scott had his own back in 1972 when he finished ahead of Roberts in the rookie Expert season and he has finished second to Roberts on two other occasions since, in the 1974 Grand National Championship, and in the 1973 series as well, when he was left well behind on both occasions.

Gary Scott won the 1975 Championship at the San Jose Mile flat track meeting on September 21st, when it was accepted that there was no way that Kenny Roberts was going to be able to beat him in spite of bringing out the massive TZ750 engine dirt bike which had scared the pants off everyone towards the latter end of the season. His fourth place at San Jose gave Scott the title but it didn't please him one little bit to win the Championship with a fourth place. In fact Gary was reported to have retreated from Press and cameras after what he considered a disappointing season.

Born in Gabriel, California on January 19th 1952, Scott moved to Springfield, Ohio over the '74/75 winter, to be nearer to the Harley-Davidson factory and the Eastern Region dirt track meetings. He ran in a few early non-National races to get used to the different combinations of engines and frames but lost to Roberts at the opening National at Houston. He then had to miss the Daytona 200 due to the completely non-competitive Harley-Davidson but, in the end, it wasn't too much of a tragedy, as Roberts fell out of the race with clutch failure, so that he gained no points either. The Dallas meeting was another disappointment when he lost to the Harley-Davidson newcomer Greg Sassamana, after a race long battle that deprived Gary of the 165 points he would have taken for a win. At Louisville, Gary was third behind yet another pair of Harleys, Springsteen and Keener, a position which he repeated at Harrington, Delaware. In spite of his somewhat lowly positions it was enough to edge him in front of Roberts, who was having considerable problems with the new Yamahas. When he won at Columbus the following week, he opened up a considerable points advantage over Roberts. At Castle Rock he finished fifth, for him a poor position as he had managed to win there twice in three years. He used a different front tyre and just about managed to qualify for the final. Gary won at Ascot but the race should have been Roberts', who, starting from the back of the field, whistled into a commanding lead which he increased from lap to lap until the rear chain fell off. The new 500 racer had been shipped from Italy in time for the Laguna Seca 75 mile road race, but its uncompetitiveness allowed him only thirteenth place in a race which Roberts won, lapping the lowly Scott twice in the process.

The TT Steeplechase at Peoria followed, where he could only manage seventh place, due to suspension problems, and he was placed in twelfth position at Santa Fe. A third place at Terre Haute elevated his points a little, in spite of the fact that he rode the race without a clutch. Roberts brought out the surprise of the season at Indianapolis in a terrible effort to close the points gap that was worrying the Yamaha camp. It turned out to be a TZ750 flat tracker on which he blew everyone off, the sheer pace of the machine causing grave concern amongst riders, factories and officials alike. Only Roberts could have ridden it but frankly Roberts didn't really want to know. The bike scared him as well! Gary suffered gearbox problems at Syracuse but finished seventh and at Toledo half-mile he claimed a second. A win would have made him champion. His fifth place at San Jose ended his chase for the Championship title. The tail end of the season was a complete disappointment. At Ascot he finished tenth and he blew out of the Ontario road race when his clutch cable broke and he damaged the gearbox racing without it!

So the 1974 runner-up came out of the 1975 season on top and goes into 1976 as America's number one rider. It was a consistent season that took Gary to the top, but a disappointing one that gave him only two wins in the process. He hopes to do better in 1976, where the competition between himself and the irrepressible Roberts should take on a new meaning. There's no way that Gary is going to give up his plate and that's all there is to it!

Champions' gallery

Mert Lawwill from Tilbourn, California. AMA Grand National Champion in 1969

The first rider to achieve the Grand Slam — Dick Mann on the machine which he dirt-tracked in his 1971 win

Daytona winner Don Emde was more used to dirt tracks than tarmac and put up some very fine performances on the former before extending his prowess to road racing. Note the steel shoe

American half-mile racing — Harley-Davidson team riders Mert Lawwill (7) and now retired Mark Brelsford (87) are among the start line line-up at famed Ascot Speedway, Los Angeles

Dave Aldana with the factory backed Norton 750 at Ascot. Note the rev counter on the handlebars

'Big bike' action at Ontario, California in 1971. Cal Rayborn (H-D 14), Kenny Roberts (350 Yamaha 60), Cliff Carr (750 Kawasaki 26) and Kel Carruthers (350 Yamaha 73) blast off from the front row of the grid. Wily race winner John Cooper isn't to be seen at this stage

Roberts in close action forgetting what two handlebars are there for!

Cal Rayborn never made National Champion, but was always a threat on the dirt

When you have time to look round, you are either well out in front or about to be overtaken!

One of the rare pictures of Gary's most able challenger, ex-Champion Roberts seen here aboard the TZ 750 Yamaha dirt tracker

12 A year with Suzuki

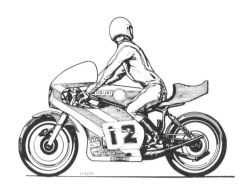

All in a twist. The man who started and ended the season in the same way!

It is not often in the world of racing that superlatives can be penned without fear of contradiction. My visit to the Suzuki factory in the early 'sixties was impressive and the standard of welcome almost beyond normal belief. It was an occasion long cherished and one which Shunzo Suzuki himself said was "almost a family occasion for him." The attitude of Suzuki has little changed during the last decade and it is with personal fondness that I remember the banquet provided at an hotel just outside Hamamatsu; a banquet of roast beef and Yorkshire pudding — a rare tribute and a lasting impression of a family firm that made the effort to please their guests.

Their welcome didn't take in the competition department, much to my everlasting regret, but they did make a point of apologising for their lack of manners! They had already entered competition on two wheels in 1960 with their first appearance at the TT. You'll have to struggle hard to find the name of Suzuki since the machines were entered under Colleda, the model rather than the make. Originally a textile company, the economic recession forced a change of attitude and the factory was re-established to cope with the need for cheap commuter transport, a decision which was to establish the Company as one of the main driving forces in the world of motorcycle sport for fifteen years, apart from a lapse when they retired from racing at the end of the 1968 season. During this period they have enlarged upon their knowledge and have been rewarded with success on a scale which few thought possible in the early sixties. Few, that is, apart from the Suzuki people themselves who made a point of honour of equipping themselves with not only the best of riders, but also the best of machinery as well, particularly after their disappointing positions in their first TT. Bad luck dogged them the following year, even though their team included South African Paddy Driver and Hughie Anderson, New Zealand's first world champion. Neither 125 nor 250 machines held together for long. Their fortunes changed when East German Ernst Degner joined them amidst a political howl. Ernst had been responsible for much of the development of the MZ which gave him a commanding appreciation of two-stroke engines and the preparation necessary to race in International competition. His slight stature made him, like Hughie, an obvious choice for the 50cc machines and he won the world 50cc championship in 1962. Through their titanic struggle with Honda, and then more latterly Yamaha as well, Suzuki built up a supreme racing organisation, adding to their riders Austrian Bertie Schneider, England's Frank Perris, and West German Hans-Georg Anscheidt to fortify their Japanese riders. Mitsuo Itoh was the first Japanese rider to win a TT and Toshio Fujii the first Japanese rider to appear on the mainland of Great Britain under team captain Frank Perris's command. His meteoric progress won the Mellano Trophy at Silverstone.

In 1964 Suzuki produced the first of their 250cc square four machines, which was basically two 125s married together. It never really worked and suffered from overheating on the two rear cylinders, which caused them to seize more often than not. Ernst Degner had been badly burned at the Japanese Grand Prix and it was with the 50 and 125 machines that Suzuki continued their major run of success. Anscheidt took the world 50cc titles in 1966, 1967 and 1968; repeating titles which had been won by Degner in 1962 and Anderson in both 1963 and 1964. Hughie also split the Honda monopoly of the 125 world championship by winning the 1963 and 1965 titles, removing them from the incredible little Swiss Honda rider Luigi Taveri, who regained his title in 1966. Suzuki also took the constructor's title no less than eight times.

With such a pedigree it is little surprising that Suzuki are back on top today, thanks to that same friendly and approachable attitude which has always been the hallmark of their operation both in Japan, Europe and the United States. But of all years, 1975 seems to have been the most memorable; memorable for not only the team's success in Europe but for one man alone — Barry Sheene. To most of the followers of motorcycle sport throughout the world, Barry personifies the new face of a growing sport. His unabashed devilment and natural skills have made him the most popular figure of all-time, and, not unnaturally, many people look upon him as Suzuki itself. He has survived a monumental pile-up at Daytona when his rear tyre gave way, returning just a few months later in true Gary Nixon fashion to take the world's fastest circuits apart with cool, determined aggression. Only ill-luck put him out of the hunt for his major championship chase, the FIM's Formula 750 title, which he won in 1973, when he broke a leg whilst fooling around in typical fashion on a paddock bike. Medical opinion suggests that the leg was already part broken but even that fact doesn't hide the tragedy of a season which started and ended in the same fashion, even if many of us did crease ourselves with idotic laughter when the news leaked through. The mirth was misplaced when we realised how serious it was, but Barry remained completely unflustered as is his philosophy on life, a philosophy which only Dave Aldana appears to have shaken in any way during some of the more engaging off-circuit situations!

Barry's spill, in practice at Daytona, was a supreme disappointment for the Suzuki team who had engaged

just about the best riders who were available to them to attack the superiority of Yamaha. Suzuki had Stan
Woods fresh out of England for his first visit, Teppi Lansivouri from Finland and, of course, the legendary Gary
Nixon. Gary was still suffering with his broken arm, as the screws holding it together were pulling away from the
bone, which made him an eventual non-runner. Dave Aldana, Hurley Wilvert and Pat Hennen were to reinforce
the team, along with two Dutch riders Rob Bron and Marcel Ankone. Those lucky enough to have the latest 1975
models included the two Dutchmen but Stan Woods had to satisfy himself with the 1974 model which was some
42 pounds heavier. Gloom had descended on the camp with the knowledge that preparations had to go ahead,
even with Barry locked away in the Halifax hospital, and for Stan Woods, double gloom, when he realized that he
had to race on Goodyear tyres after Dunlop's withdrawal from the race, following the second crash by Henk
Klassen. Goodyear's different profile required a slightly altered technique.

Chain stretch problems had haunted most competititors, not the least of whom were the Suzuki riders.
Some modifications had been made to the swinging arm on Stan's machine and with the employment of an
American chain and tensioner on recommendation from the factory, Rex White and his team thought they had
the problem licked. Practice went well with Stan qualifying in the second wave, not too disappointing in view of
his necessary familiarisation programme, a must for every new competitor using the Daytona banking for the first
time. It was expected that Stan would improve as the race itself progressed. As it happened, Stan's hopes of
doing anything in the race were dashed when he returned to the pits to have his chain adjusted, only to be excluded by an AMA official who noticed that the adjustment caused the profile of the tyre to foul the chain adjuster.
Teppi Lansivouri was also in trouble with chain stretch and he, too, had to return to the pits whilst well up on the
leader board. Rapid adjustments sent him back into the race but the effort of regaining his position was a little too
much for him and he fell off. Teppi's ability had impressed everyone during qualifying, where he finished second
fastest to the fleet Kenny Roberts at almost 110mph. Fortunately Teppi wasn't hurt but the air was blue for a
while with a few strongly felt Finnish words, muttered from under his moustache. The machine was quite badly
damaged.

Unlike the British machines, Suzuki of America had a different colour scheme. Dave Aldana at speed

Refuelling became a bit of a headache. Suzuki GB were of the opinion that all the Suzukis would be refuelled from just one tower, since it was all a bit of a one factory effort. Instead, the Americans had two towers for their own team, Suzuki GB had to make do with the Americans' last year's one, and the poor Dutchman had to use dump-cans. Popular team-manager Rex White didn't have enough staff and had to borrow the services of Eddie Crooks and Colin Seeley, who were over at Daytona on holiday. Mutual friend Mike Bradbrook also gave a helping hand. The opportunity for practice really didn't exist, the only real try-out with fuel coming during the warm-up laps prior to the start of the race. Stan was refuelled perfectly during one of his pit stops to sort out the chain, but the American team, under whose banner Teppi was riding, knocked the board man off his feet and sent tools and petrol flying all over the place. At one point even a breather pipe and catch tank flew into the British camp's pit, narrowly missing one of the team members. Short of mechanics, Suzuki GB had already had to borrow one of Merv Wright's friends to help out their efforts, a very able and competent chap by the name of Bob Fisher. Having acted as a mechanic under similar circumstances once before at Daytona, this airline pilot proved a life-saver.

It is a matter of record that all the Suzukis blew out during a race which saw the first sixteen machines home bearing the three crossed tuning forks of Yamaha. But there was better news of Barry Sheene, who had recovered enough to listen to the race on the hospital radio. Barry's operation had been successful and Suzuki were able to fly him home five days later. With a broken leg and ribs plus other inconvenient accoutrements, he was man-handled from Daytona to Miami in Bill France's own private aircraft, where he boarded a 747 for Heathrow and where a jet helicopter picked him up and dropped him on his own front lawn at Wisbech. US Suzuki team manager, Merv Wright, accompanied him on his tedious trip home and I am sure all those at Halifax Hospital were glad to see the last of Barry and his hoard of friends!

The absence of Barry for the prestigious Imola event left both Stan Woods and John Newbold in the hot seats. Stan had taken delivery of a 1975 model but had not managed to cover himself with too much glory at Mallory Park during the first of the Match Races by bending it, falling off at Devil's Elbow. The chain problems

Suzuki GB team manager with the three works machines for 1975

had been solved but the choice of crankshafts made the preparation of the machines for the actual race a bone of contention. Lightweight crankshafts had been made available at Daytona to enable the engine to rev higher, but this only seemed to allow more vibration. The factory were there with Teppi and joined forces with Suzuki GB for refuelling — which again produced a few fireworks. John Newbold was to ride a 1974 model but he failed to make much of an impression in practice, which was completely dominated by Lansivouri on the 120bhp machine. Stan was eighth fastest, behind a whole row of Yamahas splitting the Kawasakis of Ditchburn and DuHamel. Unlike the Daytona 200, the Imola classic was split into two separate races so it was an all-out effort to secure advantage in both. Again hopes took a tumble when Stan Woods crashed in the first leg, removing more skin and further injuring the finger which he damaged at Mallory Park. John rode to a superb ninth place on a three year old machine, but was unable to manage any but last in the second leg, due to the lack of a front brake, not the best of things to be without at Imola. John's mechanic, Martyn, had been experiencing a great deal of trouble with the brake and literally ran out of time to get it right before the second leg. Since it was John's first ride in a Formula 750 race, no one was too disappointed.

The refuelling stop, so much of a problem at Daytona, was relatively easy at Imola. Suzuki had plenty of people to help and hard practice got it right for the first leg. When Teppi crashed, endeavouring to hold his lead against a rapidly closing Agostini, the Japanese team cleared right out of the pits, leaving one Oriental to help refuel. But a little bit of help from friends saved the day yet again, and with Lansivouri remounted, the occasion passed without mishap. Lansivouri finished second in this first race but burnt his clutch out at the start of the second, and retired after six laps, when holding eighth position. It was another walk-over for Yamaha, but John managed to finish fifteenth, on aggregate.

The team arrived at Mettet in June, with very high hopes. By now Barry was fit and had ridden at Brands Hatch and Mallory Park with success and notched two new lap records at Brands, the fastest during the *Evening News* 15 lap Invitation event at 85.19mph. Two weeks later he had taken the Grand Prix 500 to Chimay where he astounded even himself with a record breaking ride, beating Phil Read by some 35 seconds and setting a fastest

Irresistible, the finest rider of the British and European year — Barry Sheene riding under his lucky number 7

lap of 128mph. The 750 had presented problems with the exhaust pipe starting to crack. John had been riding well at the Grand Prix events and at the home meets, and was itching to get back on the big 750. Stan had crashed badly at Brands Hatch, breaking his knee-cap and wrist, but as he expected to be fit for Assen, Rex White had brought the whole team to Belgium. All the bikes were there and as many spares and equipment as could be carried in the Bedford and one Transit. This time the team was to be away from their base at Croydon for two months, arriving back in England in time for the August Brands Hatch meeting. By now the team was equipped with four 1975 models — two for Barry and one each for Stan and John — plus last year's machines to be used as spares in case anything untoward happened.

Barry won the first leg, in spite of his pipes splitting, but in the second race the pipes actually broke in half and he was forced to retire when some thirty seconds in the lead. John finished well in sixth place overall, after a brilliant ride in the second race where he took second place behind Dave Potter and in front of first race winner Patrick Pons. Even this result was affected by the fact that he had lost a tail pipe in the first race, where he could manage no better than thirteenth, along with the added inconvenience of having to change gear with a short stub after the gear lever fell apart!

A week later the team was at Magny Cours, the 2.39 mile circuit near Nevers in central France, where the holiday camp atmosphere allows spectators to actually camp in the paddock, unheard of almost everywhere else. The organisers provide huge piles of wood and the evenings evolve into wine parties round camp fires. Fortunately Suzuki had obtained a pit garage and created their own private area in which to work on the machines undisturbed, away from the temptation of all that booze! They had also resisted the temptation to rush back to England to get Barry's 1974 machine, for the problem of the splitting pipes was beginning to haunt them. Although Barry won pole position for the race they found that the splitting continued and decided to make some spare sets so that they could be changed during the interval between the two races as became necessary. Barry had already won, the two previous years he had ridden, setting lap records into the bargain, so he was obviously favourite to win yet again. Since Barry is a national hero in France, most of the pre-race publicity was on him — and stayed on him as he unrolled yet another astonishing set of records.

Like all people who learned to race two-strokes the hard way, team rider John Newbold carefully poises with his finger over the clutch lever

Barry shot off into an early confrontation with his close friend Johnny Cecotto, being joined by Estrosi, DuHamel and Pons. Newbold was having a little battle of his own further down the field. When he came in to refuel no fuel came through the quick filler so he was sent out to do a few more laps while the problem was solved. It transpired that the jubilee clips holding the tap to the hose had turned round, fouling the valve handle. John was recalled for fuel and sent out again to rejoin the fray. Next it was Barry's turn, and alarm was swept into the team when Barry refused to take any notice of the board. At first they thought he hadn't seen it, but the truth of the matter was that Barry was enjoying himself so much that he didn't want to spoil it. He came in a few laps later and, having been fuelled, rejoined the race to regain his lead. But it was obvious that both he and John had split exhaust pipes, in spite of heavy welding, which would need repairing or replacing before the second race. John eventually lost his tail pipe.

In between races the mechanics slaved away to get both machines ready for the second race. In fact so close a call was it that Barry arrived on the line after the warm-up lap had commenced. Barry had to finish within twenty-three seconds of Estrosi, who had finished second to him in the first 95.6 mile leg, but as he had always liked to get the bit between his teeth and win convincingly, he waltzed away with the second race, there being no more than 0.1mph difference between his two race speeds. His second race produced a new lap record of 89.14mph, at the end of which Barry was worn out. John managed fifth place and that night there was the biggest celebration ever.

The Suzuki team arrived at Anderstorp a week before the race, which was due to take place on July 19th. It wasn't really worth returning to England after the Belgian Grand Prix, which had been a little disappointing to the team. Barry had shown his mastery of the very rapid circuit, but after passing Phil Read and Giacomo Agostini for the lead, his machine had slowed and he was eventually forced to retire after setting a new lap record on the 500 four of 135.51mph. John Newbold was rapidly proving his ability and took second place behind Read, gaining his second world championship points. The organisers were already at the circuit, and helped no end to obtain a power supply and send telex messages to England to assist in getting parts for the quite luxurious Motorhomes, which have been a large visual part of the Suzuki organisation since the beginning of 1975. Not

October at Brands Hatch saw a few changes including Phil Read out on Barry's machine. A start fracas eliminated Phil, as it did many other riders

long after they arrived and set up camp, Yamaha put in an appearance for a private test session and were a little chagrined to find they had been preceded by the opposition. However, a pretence at non-interest eventually persuaded Yamaha that there were no ill-wishes, even if stop watches were concealed in pockets!

The whole area was on holiday, so no shops or restaurants were open to provide some of the more standard joys of being abroad. Yamaha couldn't find anything to eat or drink so they had to knuckle under to being entertained by Suzuki, with Agostini insisting that his mechanic act as food taster — a not unnaturally enjoyable task for him. As the rest of the riders arrived it became increasingly obvious that everything in the garden was not rosy. Start money problems reared their ugly heads, not for the first time, and it was assumed that the organisers considered that, as riders were at Anderstorp for the Grand Prix the day after the F750 races, they were going to get away with poor payment for the 750 race. There were threats and counterthreats with Cecotto and Sheene quite rightly leading the revolt. Cecotto eventually refused to ride, but after urgent calls back to England, Barry had to take his position on the grid following team orders. With the increase in start money demanded by the riders, Stan Woods was refused an entry on the basis that he wasn't 100% certain, and Rex White had to ring him in England to give him the bad news. It was intended that Stan would fly out to join the team at Anderstorp if he was fit enough.

Having just completed two Grand Prix events the 750 machines needed looking at quite closely as their appearances gave a sorrowful sight. The exhaust pipes were still causing trouble but the mechanics had worked out a way of mounting and strengthening them to give a slightly longer life and enough, hopefully, to last a one hundred mile leg. The pits looked as though they would give refuelling problems. Formula One criteria had meant that the old ones had gone, giving place to a superb set of pits which, though great for car drivers, were not so good for motorcyclists. The pits consisted of a raised spectator gallery and white lines painted between the support pillars divided the area into about twenty bays, at an angle of forty-five degrees to the pit road. Riders left the circuit about one hundred yards before the bend approaching the pits, entering by the back road, and then swinging right-handed through the pits to get back onto the circuit. Rex and Jackie White considered that the best pit was the first one and were up early on race morning to claim squatters' rights. This ensured that

Amongst the new names in the Suzuki line-up for 1976 will be that of Percy Tait, who had a try out at Brands Hatch

Teppi Lansivuori has a reputation for falling off at most meetings, and this selection of photographs proves that the September Race of the Year was no exception. His final indignity was a lift back to the paddock behind Barry Sheene

a minimum of time was lost refuelling but had its disadvantages in that any rider overshooting the entrance would end up in their pit!

The first leg got off to a good start with Teppi in a familiar leading position from Barry for the first sixteen laps, after which they changed places until refuelling. From then on Teppi couldn't catch Barry, even though he put in the fastest lap in the process. John Newbold was struggling to hold eighth place but his pit stop relegated him to twelfth, finishing two laps down on the leaders. Again he hit trouble with his exhaust pipes.

For the second leg there developed a ding-dong battle between Barry, Teppi and Barry Ditchburn with the lead changing constantly until Teppi's crankshaft failed and he was forced to relinquish the chase on the ninth lap. Ditchburn won the second leg by 0.029 seconds, but Barry's second place gave him the event, along with fastest lap and a new lap record. John Newbold was going very well in fifth and sixth places until an oil seal breakage on the crankshaft forced his retirement on the twenty-second lap. This was something quite new to Suzuki and the realisation effectively shortened the crankshaft life by 50%. From then on the crankshafts were changed much more frequently but the factory were found to be out of stock, so arrangements had to be made to have them rebuilt in England. After this there was an endless procession of crankshafts being transported to and from Derby from the Suzuki base at Croydon.

After being away from home for so long, the return trip promised to be quite relaxing, but a storm blew up between Gothenberg and Tilbury and most of the team spent their time just lying in their bunks, not up to the rather delicious Smorgasbord freely available for the whole trip. The landing was effected quite without mishap and after the customary delay with searches in the Custom's shed, the team headed for Croydon with but three days before the next event. Barry's success at Anderstorp had also included a victory in the Grand Prix itself, where he beat his two closest rivals, Phil and Giacomo. He clipped almost three seconds off the record.

Silverstone was next on the list with the two legs of the FIM Championship run on two separate days, making it much easier for everyone. This was Britain's round of the championship and the heat was really on in almost tropical weather and in front of a home-crowd. Again the pits were brand new after having been built for the British Grand Prix, and only after a search did the realisation dawn that the impressive array of non-working power points could only be made to work by starting the generator! This was quite okay, but no-one seemed to know who was in charge of it, and it was to be the focal point of many misunderstandings and problems. It was started very late on Thursday night, and with some teams with quite a lot of work to do on their machines there was a reluctance to turn it off. The big generator therefore plonked its way through the night, destroying everyone's beauty sleep and leading to a re-arrangement of hours for Friday night, when it was agreed that it should be turned off at midnight. This worked perfectly, but someone walked off with the starting key and no power was to be had for the Saturday, until very late in the day. That evening the generator stopped quite early so everyone went to bed to enjoy a good night's sleep. But it transpired that this also provided the electricity to the public camp site where a disco was in progress, and a riot ensued, the result of which was not particularly happy. The generator had run out of fuel!

Saturday's star was undoubtedly Cecotto, whose fast and furious riding took him to a well deserved win ahead of Patrick Pons, Teppi and Barry. He almost cast the race aside when he fell off in the pits during his refuelling stop, but his mechanics got him sorted out very quickly and back into the race. John Newbold suffered from a bad mix-up at the startline gate where some marshals thought there was to be a warm-up lap and consequently held back part of the field to stagger the numbers onto the course. A warm-up lap there wasn't and by the time John got onto the circuit, the race was started. Aware that there was no way that he could catch up, John retired from the race.

The second race on Sunday caused possibly the biggest sensation of the year. Cecotto had asked the works Yamaha team for the loan of a spare engine as his was a little worse for wear, but they delayed a decision until it was too late to fit it before the race. After much argument with Yamaha, he told Barry of his problem and it was suggested that he borrow Teppi's spare machine. This machine was not set up properly as Teppi hadn't bothered with it during practice and Johnny lasted only five laps before the head gasket blew. With Cecotto mounted on a Suzuki instead of his Yamaha the sparks really flew and it was confidently predicted that the promised works' contract with Yamaha would not transpire for 1976. Again this second race had been a close one, but it settled down to a real match between Ditchburn on the very fast works Kawasaki and Barry Sheene, with the lead changing constantly. Both riders even refuelled on the same lap, which was quite a sight to behold. Barry nearly demolished an over-keen member of Ditchburn's pit crew. The result went to Barry, with Teppi filling third place behind Ditchburn. This gave the overall result to Sheene and another valuable fifteen points.

John Williams had a superb outing on the Suzuki at Brands Hatch ...

His winning record average was 109.99mph and he stood sixteen points clear of the next man in the table.

By the time of the Assen meeting on September 6th the inimitable Sheene had also won at Oulton Park by more than a minute and with the first 100mph lap of the circuit. He had also taken the 500 to Pesaro and again beaten Agostini with yet another lap record into the bargain. But Assen was not to be a continuation of his success and marked the end of his championship chase. A win here would have clinched the title, but mechanical problems added no further points, and Barry's unfortunate spill at Cadwell Park during the following weeks ended any hopes that he might have had.

Unlike the situation at the Grand Prix, Assen was empty, with no fans milling around the town; in fact they didn't arrive until just before the race, a most unreal situation for the infamous Assen, where the jails are always cleared out in anticipation of the Grand Prix crowds! It was a very different atmosphere as the team settled down in the paddock, in anticipation of yet another successful weekend, but problems set in during practice when Barry blew up an engine necessitating a frantic rebuild before the race itself. All three riders were at the meeting and Teppi also turned up, but didn't race, due to an argument on the question of start money. All three riders put in good practice times and slicks were fitted for the first race. Storm clouds blew up and heavy rain threatened but fortunately never materialised. Barry shot off to a fantastic start and was well ahead of the two Kawasakis of Ditchburn and DuHamel until just after the refuelling stop when the engine started misfiring. The trouble was soon found: the petrol pipe to the carburettor had become dislodged and Barry was able to slip it back on sufficiently to get him back to the pits. The mechanics put the matter right and Barry went out again, but misfiring continued and again he returned to the pits, only to have his father Frank send him back out again to continue the race as best he could. By now he was well down on the rest of the field and it was not apparent if he would be disqualified from the race after his second pit stop. The machine was running badly and as he was still without much of a chance of getting back into the running, Barry called it a day and retired from the race. Ditchburn and DuHamel took over the running but 'Ditch' ran out of fuel just before the end and it was DuHamel's race. John managed to take eighth place and Stan finished seventeenth.

... quickly getting used to the strange machine and leading John Newbold who found he had to take a back seat most of the way round

No, not Gary Nixon!

For the second leg Barry led for the first three laps, but then felt the engine tighten. An experienced two-stroke rider, he pulled in rather than risk the almost fatal consequences of a seizure. After inspection it was found that the slide peg in the centre carburettor had sheered allowing the slide to turn round, causing petrol starvation. John Newbold had, by now, got himself into a massive scrap and finished second to DuHamel, who had turned in one of the best performances of his career. This second place gave John a third place overall, with the Australian Jack Findlay taking second place. This elevated Jack into a chance for the Championship with the final round at Hockenheim to come.

Rex White and his team prepared for Hockenheim with a lack of real enthusiasm. Barry had broken his leg whilst playing about on a paddock bike and thus Jack Findlay had to take points from either of the first three positions to win the overall FIM Championship. There was still concern over Stan's fitness and the important aspect of keeping machines ahead of Findlay — and thus ensure that it became Barry's title — was of paramount importance for Suzuki. With only John as serious opposition Rex White decided to ask John Williams to ride Barry's machine with the hope that Suzuki could fill two of the three important places. Although there were many other good riders at the meeting there could be no guarantee that they would be able to relegate Jack Findlay to lower than third place and it became a case of an effort to help themsleves. There was also a rumour floating around that Barry had offered rather a lot of money to any rider who could finish in front of Jack, but the validity of such a rumour was never correctly established.

On short circuits Barry Ditchburn came closest to taking Barry's titles from him and remained the biggest threat throughout. Here he is winning the Post TT in June

Since the Insermini days, France hasn't quite been able to produce star riders. Now they have at least four, the best probably being Patrick Pons, seen here during the 1975 Dutch F750 race as Assen. Pons completed the 1975 season by winning at Hockenheim and coming third in the overall FIM F750 championship behind Findlay and Sheene

Practice was difficult, to say the least. It rained constantly, so a choice of tyres was difficult to assess. The machines gave no problems so it looked as though the efforts throughout the year had proven successful. Like all two-strokes, setting the carburation was a problem in that at Hockenheim in September the weather changed from being hot during the day to cold in the morning. As the race was due to start at 8.00 am, but with practice during the warmer parts of the day, there was little opportunity to gauge the jetting needed for the race itself. It was a position familiar to all two-stroke riders and one which had caused no end of arguments at our own TT for countless years. In spite of the fact that John Williams hadn't ridden the Suzuki before he gained pole position, even in the rain! After what is commonly an almost constant ritual of argument over one point or another with the organisers, the Hockenheim chiefs saw sense and the start of the race was put forward to 9.00 am. Moving it by an hour presented the other problem that the two hour break between both legs of the race was reduced to one hour, and thus any problems which may have been encountered during the first race left little time to sort out before the second.

Early on race day or, as the Germans would put it, Fruh am Morgen, saw the usual sight of the Suzuki team creeping down to cadge the best position for the refuelling tower before other riders were up and about. This was again accomplished successfully and hopes were raised by the news that Barry's operation had proved a success.

On the first lap of the first race, dutifully at 9.00 am, John Newbold lay fourth, John Williams eighth and Stan Woods about seventeenth, not very pleased with his front brake, a discontentment which caused him to retire by the ninth lap. John Williams continued to work his way through the field until he was second, but by this time John Newbold was having trouble with his choice of tyres and was in eighth place, where he finished the race. Newbold had chosen intermediate tyres whilst the others went for slicks! Williams also finished in second place behind Patrick Pons, but with Jack Findlay third, things looked bad for Suzuki. Between races Jack had to bandage his exhaust pipes, a job which was completed by his mechanic, Derek Booth, in the nick of time.

Patrick Pons shot off into a lead in the second race and both Johns settled down to second and third positions. All three were riding brilliantly and the Suzuki twosome only changed positions during the refuelling stop, after which they settled once more into Williams second and Newbold third. At one point it looked as though Williams might catch Pons but this was a bit of a forlorn hope. Dieter Braun, filling fourth place between Newbold and Findlay was a valuable asset to Suzuki for, if he remained there, the title would go to Barry languishing in hospital. On the twelfth lap Dieter retired with a broken chain and Jack was able to finish fourth. There had been frantic calculations going on in the Suzuki pit to see what the final position would be if the two Johns were changed round, giving Newbold more points, but no paper mathematics could produce other than the obvious result that Jack's points for both races gave him third overall and thus the Championship. Natural disappointment at losing the title was over-ruled by Jack's win. His popularity within the world of big bike racing had never been higher and, after all, he used to be a Suzuki rider with Saaid!

The year thus ended in failure at Hockenheim, but failure only in gaining the much sought FIM title. The crowd loved John Williams and were delighted to see him on board Barry's machine. After returning from Germany, the Race of the South at Brands Hatch in October provided John Williams with a winning ride, but this meeting was rather marred by the multiple pile-up which saw Phil Read's first race on the Suzuki come to an end on the first lap. Suzuki took first, second and third places with Newbold second and Percy Tait third. Williams also put up a new outright lap record at 95.20mph.

Suzuki GB march into 1976 confident of success. Whilst other teams appear to have rather a lot of changes planned, not all of them voluntary, Suzuki hope to retain their leading riders and that includes the maestro himself. Regrettably, Merv Wright replaces Rex White as Manager, Merv suffering from a lack of a team in United States where Suzuki have withdrawn. Rex has always been one of the most approachable of people, even from his scootering days with Lambretta, and we can but wish Merv Wright the success which Rex has brought to the presentation of the team at home and abroad.

Barry Sheene's Record Year

Major Events:

March 7th — Daytona: Crashed at 175mph during practice on his 750 Suzuki

April 27th — Cadwell: Retired on 10th Lap

May 4th — Austrian Grand Prix: Pulled off starting grid at last minute by officials and banned from GP. Finished 6th during practice, on his 500 Suzuki

May 11th — W. German Grand Prix: Not placed

May 26th — Brands Hatch: 500cc (12 Laps), 1st: 10m.59s — 81.28mph, Fastest Lap: 53.2s — 83.91mph (Record) Evening News 1000cc (15 Laps), 1st: 13m.21.6s — 83.53mph Record Lap: Grant & Sheene 52.4s — 85.19mph

June 1st — Belgium Grand Prix: 500cc (10 Laps), 1st: 28m.50.22s, Lap Record: 2m.48.14s — 126.3mph

June 8th — Mallory Park: Record Lap: 500cc Heats — Read & Sheene, 1000cc — Finished 8th

June 15th — Mettet: First Leg: 2nd, Second Leg: Retired, Fastest Lap: 2m.16.1s — 128.95mph (Record)

June 22nd — Magnycours: First Leg: (40 Laps) 95.6 miles, 1st: 1hr.5m.10.34s — 86.81mph, Record Lap: 1m.35.3s — 89.17mph, Second Leg: (40 Laps), 1st: 1hr.5m.8.71s — 86.85mph, Record Lap: 1m.35.25s — 89.14mph

June 28th — Dutch TT: 500cc (16 Laps), 1st: 48.01.0s — 95.69mph, Fastest Lap: 2m.55.5s — 98.14mph (Record)

July 6th — Belgium Grand Prix: 500cc — Not placed, Fastest Lap: 3m.52.2s — 135.75mph (Record)

July 20th — Swedish Grand Prix: 500cc — 1st: 48m.30.69s — 86.38mph, Fastest Lap: 1m.41.35s — 88.19mph (Record)

July 27th — Finnish Grand Prix: Retired

August 9th & 10th British GP: First Leg — Saturday: 4th (750cc), 57m.27.8s — 106.97mph. Second Leg — Sunday: 1st (750cc), 56m.25.2s — 108.99mph. 1000cc: 3rd (500cc), 24m.39.4s — 106.84mph, Overall Positions: 1st

August 17th — Pesaro Road Races: 500cc: 1st (No time given)

August 28th — Czech Grand Prix: Retired

September 7th — Assen: First Leg: Retired, Fastest Lap: 2m.56.1s, Second Leg: Retired, Outright Lap Record: 2m.54.9s — 98.4mph

September 14th — Race of the Year: 1st — 33m.46.4s, Record Lap: 49.4s — 98.39mph. 500cc: 1st —13m.25.0s — 90.56mph. MCN Superbike Champ: 1st, 21m.14.4s — 95.33mph, Fastest Lap: Sheene & Grant 49.8s — 97.59mph

Amongst other rivals were Mick Grant and Phil Read, who themselves fought a close battle at Brands Hatch

Undeniably the finest of road racers and probably the one person the crowds flock to see most of all. Having escaped death at Daytona in an accident which would probably have written-off less a mortal, Barry Sheene took only three months to recover before he returned to the saddle to shatter race and lap records throughout Europe. His Cockney manner and easy-going nature allows him to enjoy life to its full

Some of the best

It almost seems as though Australian Jack Findlay has been around since racing began! Because he still rides with a French Licence and used to live in Italy, many were those who could never quite work out his nationality. One of the nicest of all road racers, Jack has always taken success and defeat with a peculiarly Australian grace. Whoever might take his 1975 FIM title from him will have an awful lot to live up to

The great American all-rounder Kenny Roberts. Twice AMA Grand National Champion in 1973 and 1974, Kenny is probably the finest road racer in the world today. Twenty four years of age from Orange County, California he stands a mere 5½ feet tall but looks a giant on board the yellow and black Yamaha. He finished runner-up to Gary Scott in the 1975 league but claims that his title has only gone out on loan!

The greatest of all world champions with more scalps to his belt than any other, Giacomo Agostini regained his senior crown at the conclusion of the 1975 series but, apart from wins at Imola, Daytona and Paul Ricard in 1974, hasn't performed too well on a 750 since. He made his debut as a road racer in 1962 at an Italian National event on a Morini and has since won fifteen world titles. Joined Yamaha in 1974 straight from MV to whose camp he has now returned. Aged 33, his hobbies are water skiing, off-road riding and ordinary skiing

Yvon DuHamel, with or without his beard, is one of the hard men of the world's circuits. More often than not supreme Canadian champion on tarmac and snow, Yvon has achieved a reputation for being ready and willing to ride anything anywhere and at any time. Quite often he wins but also suffers his crashes more often than others

Gene Romero from San Luis Obispo, California, achieved the notable distinction of winning the 1975 Daytona 200. He also captured Mike Hailwood's one hour record put up on the same Daytona circuit. 1970 Grand National Champion he first made headlines in 1968 by winning the Lincoln, Nebraska TT, finishing that season seventh ranked in the United States. Since that time he has rarely been out of the top ten places. Yamaha took Gene into their team in 1974 when he returned the favour by winning at Indianapolis, Indiana and Ontario. Born in Martinez in May 1947, Gene stays at the top of his profession in 1976, but is unlikely to have works Yamahas available to him outside of the United States

After an encouraging fourth place at the Daytona 200 in 1974, Don Castro has risen in the ranks of road racing abilities. He joined Yamaha in 1973 and carried the number eleven plate in 1975. Born on December 28 1949, he comes from Hollister, California. He commenced racing in 1968 and turned professional in 1970

Born in Paris on December 24 1952, Patrick Pons started his career in April 1971 at the Monthlery ten hour race. His first victory came at Reims in June the same year and he has steadfastly improved to record probably his finest victory — at Mettet in 1975 where he won the 750 round

23 year old John Newbold began racing in 1971 with his first road race at Darley Moor on a 250cc machine. Riding the ex-John Cooper Yamsel he quickly established a reputation in 1972 and broke into the big time the following year. With a whole string of wins on smaller capacity machines, John has found difficulty in matching the heavier Suzuki which he now rides. He has fast gained experience this year ending the season with a second place at Brands Hatch

Teppi Lansivuori has not had the best of seasons in America, Europe or in Britain come to that, but he has consistently been one of the fastest riders of 'big bikes' during 1975. His Grand Prix debut was in 1968 on board a 125 Montesa but he had already gained experience at ice racing in Finland and then, more latterly, on his road racing Husqvarna. Thirty years of age the flying Finn knows only one way to race and that's out at the front. Always popular around the world's circuits he says little, having no command of English and can drink Bacardi until it comes out of his ears!

Road racing has never been one of Dave Aldana's strongest points but he has staggered everyone this year by putting up some performances which have dumbfounded his critics and made the world realise what a mature and talented rider he is. He has raced in every form of competition including motocross

The most popular of American riders, Gary Nixon was one of the first to ride in Europe. He has suffered considerably from broken bones in recent years which have kept him out of the competitive saddle. AMA Grand National Champion in 1967 and 1968, he won no less than fourteen individual Nationals. A serious accident nearly ended his career in 1969 but a plucky three year comeback culminated with three straight National wins in 1973 and a third place in the National standings. A serious crash in Japan in 1974 almost finished him.

Yorkshireman Mick Grant started his career way back in 1967 with a Velocette and made his Isle of Man debut the following year. Since that era he has become one of Britain's fastest riders and broke Mike Hailwood's Isle of Man lap record during the 1975 event. Equally as quick in Ulster as on the mainland's shorter circuits, Mick nevertheless appears to prefer longer races on the more difficult circuits where he can prove his total mastership. Just topping thirty-one years of age, he certainly ranks amongst the 'older' riders and is certainly not one who takes too many risks

The first rider to break the 100mph barrier at Snetterton, Barry Ditchburn lends additional experience to the Kawasaki team in Europe. Like Mick, Barry started racing in 1967 and from 1970 until 1974 he rode Yamahas for Ted Broad. He is equally at home during long-distance races as he is during the short circuit events and has already this year won major prizes on British circuits. He is a determined rider and the one most likely to show even greater success for Kawasaki during 1976

Dave Croxford was out for the first time on the new Cosworth racer which ended up very much scratched in the ten man pile up. Brands Hatch 1975

Loop the loop! Ron Haslam riding Mallory Park's Shaws hairpin during a 1976 Match race